'Talking with God is a w   e
of the author's being. A   is
shines through the page
Rev John Ryeland, Direct

'*Talking With God* takes you on a journey that will deepen your faith and prayer life. Nigel encourages us to use Scripture and imagination to go beyond the surface and to have a deeply personal conversation with God. A great resource which is easy to use, and in which there is something for all Christians and those who truly seek a deeper relationship with God through Scripture.'
Father Peter Williams OSB, Worth Abbey

'I started to read this book slowly, one meditation at a time. The method used wasn't my natural way of praying, but to my surprise the first one brought me to tears as I revisited a memory of being filled with a sense of wonder and love as I, for the first time, saw the night sky in a place not polluted by light.

'As I entered into a dialogue with God I was further moved to hear words of tender affirmation and encouragement.

'I think the book will help many others to enter into relationship with this same God, our compassionate and life-giving Creator.'
Gina, CSF

Talking with God

Touching the beauty of God amid our chaotic world

Nigel Thonger

instant
ap◻stle

First published in Great Britain in 2023

Instant Apostle
104 The Drive
Rickmansworth
Herts
WD3 4DU

British Library Cataloguing-in-Publication Data

A catalogue record for this book is available from the British Library.

This book and all other Instant Apostle books are available from Instant Apostle:

Website: www.instantapostle.com

Email: info@instantapostle.com

ISBN 978-1-912726-67-7

Printed in Great Britain.

Contents

Acknowledgements

The book has evolved from my association with Crowhurst Christian Healing Centre (CCHC), where I often led the Christ-centred meditation at the Healing Weekends. These retreats were, and still are, great opportunities to see God at work, and they enabled ministers to learn from each other. So, to the chaplains and prayer ministers who pooled their knowledge and experience during these weekends, I express my thanks, for this has added real value to the book. I thank the Rev Steve Gendall, Senior Chaplain at CCHC, for reading the manuscript and offering suggestions that have enhanced the book in many ways. I am also indebted to my friends who reviewed the initial drafts. I confirm the contents of this book have arisen out of my own experiences and are not intended to be used to express any particular theological emphasis or belief held by CCHC.

I am most grateful to the team at Instant Apostle, Nicki Copeland, Nigel Freeman and Anne Rogers for their help and encouragement throughout the publishing process, and especially to Sheila Jacobs, who edited the book and helped me improve the manuscript with her wise and astute comments and suggestions.

I would be unable to write such a book without the constant help and guidance of the Holy Spirit and I praise

Him for His loving and gentle oversight. The wisdom in the book is all His, whereas the errors are all mine.

Last but not least, I thank my wife, Sue, for her loving support and encouragement as the book came to life.

All royalties from this book will be paid to Crowhurst Christian Healing Centre (registered charity number 208738).

Foreword
Rev Steve Gendall

God loves you.

Nigel says, 'If we focus on just one thing, we would do well to focus on the love of God.'[1]

The psalmist says, 'The earth is filled with your love, Lord.'[2]

During Her Late Majesty The Queen's address to mark the seventy-fifth anniversary of VE Day, praising Britain's response to the coronavirus epidemic, the Queen remarkably said, 'But our streets are not empty; they are filled with the love and the care that we have for each other.'[3]

Love can be expressed in many ways. With an appropriate and careful touch, an act of kindness or by laying down one's life for another; and what treasure it is to hear the sincerely spoken words, 'I love you.'

I remember well the first time I experienced God's love – I was overwhelmed and it set a course for me that I still follow today (nearly forty years later). The countless conversations with God since then have sustained, matured and guided me, disciplined and instructed me

---

[1] See Chapter 15.

[2] Psalm 119:64.

[3] www.youtube.com/watch?v=vuEf9xMmYuo (accessed 26th August 2022).

and, not least of all, taught me much about Father, Jesus and the Holy Spirit – our Triune God – and I have learned much about myself too.

I have known Nigel for nearly ten years and when I first read *Talking with God*, my heart was stirred and warmed. Not least of all because I know this is not a work Nigel would have set out on lightly or selfishly, but with conviction that God had tasked him with it. Nigel's desire to only do the Lord's bidding is a witness to his deep, strong faith in Jesus, and humility before Jesus as Lord. He is exemplary in this.

After the initial reading, I then took the plunge and chose a chapter that was applicable to my circumstances at the time. I prayerfully began to use my imagination as I read through it. A surprising thing happened! I began a conversation that was revisited between me and the Lord for more than three days. I must be honest, I was not expecting this, but what joy it brought me.

Conversation is a necessity to building our relationship with Father, Jesus and the Holy Spirit. Life has many twists and turns, much light and darkness, and a healthy relationship that includes dialogue with God is vital. But it's not only the routine of our daily lives we can talk with God about. In conversation with Him, we can experience all those things God desires to reveal to us on life's journey. There is much room for fun and adventure too (sadly, so overlooked)! We do well to make conversation with God part of our daily rhythm of life, and Nigel has given us a brilliant resource to help! There are conversation starters in this book I've never thought of and I trust they will open doors for us to see, hear and experience all that God has prepared for those who love Him.

At Crowhurst Christian Healing Centre, we regularly see the amazing and wonderful results of God encounters: burdens shifted, lives changed, people liberated and healed. God's peace and presence are all around and conversation flows. When we reach out to God, we can be sure He reaches out to us.

On reading the final draft, I noticed my imagination wandering off to the smell of freshly baked bread and a good cup of coffee. In a sense, *Talking with God* can be that stimulating – it calls out, 'Would you like to have this, this conversation with God?' Who wouldn't?! I recommend it to you – enjoy God, and believe He enjoys you!

Talking with God has been (and goes on being) saturated in prayer, with the fingerprints of God's Holy Spirit clearly evident. Give conversation with God some time, and you may be surprised where it leads.

Rev Steve Gendall
Senior Chaplain (CEO)
Crowhurst Christian Healing Centre

Introduction

The idea that people can talk with God as a friend, instead of only praying to Him in a formal setting, may seem to some a little irreverent, or even impertinent, but in essence, it is just another way of praying to God. There are books already that give advice on how to pray, and many with prayers for people and situations. We also have the Lord's Prayer as a gift from Jesus so that everyone has a template on how to start praying, and we can read testimonies and personal prayer stories from those who inspire us. Yet there is room for another book about prayer, because God is always eager to hear from His people, and with each prayer we offer, we acknowledge Him and move deeper into the love-relationship that He shares with us.

Talking with God uses informal conversation as the means for us to commune with God, a dialogue between friends who speak and listen to each other. Jesus called His disciples friends, not servants, because He shared with them everything His Father told Him.[4] He chooses us to be His friends also, and anoints us, so that we can imitate Him and achieve similar or 'greater things';[5] and He does this knowing that friendship involves an informality not

---

[4] See John 15:15.
[5] John 14:12.

found in other relationships. Therefore, since Jesus is the 'exact representation' of God,[6] it follows we can humbly revere Him in our praise and worship as Almighty God, in heaven and on earth, and also meet Him informally as friend and confidant in our prayers, and in our imagination.[7]

The aim of the book is to provide a format for the Holy Spirit to help us talk easily with God, so that we will know what He wants to say to us about various topics residing in His Word. Father and Son talked to each other often, and we are Their adopted family, so They are expecting to talk with us too, as family. A passage in St John's Gospel has Jesus saying:

> Father, I thank you that you have heard me. I knew that you always hear me, but I said this for the benefit of the people standing here.[8]

Jesus wanted to show the people standing beside Him that He could actually speak with His Father in a conversational manner, and His Father could, and did, speak with Him in the same way. Talking to God is a real divine–human experience that we can all share, wherever we are on the journey of faith, and since God is calling His people daily to follow Him, it seems natural He will want to talk with us while we are doing this.

There are thirty chapters in this book, in three groups: God and Beginnings, What is God Like? and Living the

---

[6] Hebrews 1:3.

[7] When using imagination, care must be taken. Please see comments later in this section under 'Imagining our conversation'.

[8] John 11:41-42.

Christian Life. Each topic provides opportunity for the Holy Spirit to meet us individually, where we are, and bring us closer to God. It is always the Holy Spirit who ministers to us, speaks to us and teaches us God's wisdom.

So, whatever our situation, whether life is treating us well or we're hurting, bruised and weary, waiting for relief; whether we've suffered from the deceit of the world and we're looking for truth and meaning for our life, or seeking refreshment and reassurance there is real goodness to be found on earth; or we're longing for a closer walk and deeper union with God, this book can help us, because the Spirit will bring us into conversation with Jesus. He can do this if we're walking our spiritual path in company with others, or we're walking on our own.

This makes it a book for the whole Church of God, because all who know God through the Spirit, and all who yearn to make His acquaintance, will be given God's invitation to talk, and those of us who accept it will be blessed through meeting and talking with Him. Maybe we will come to know Jesus more intimately through the Spirit, or be transformed by the closer relationship we develop with the Holy Spirit, or we will relate to Father God a little better, despite His mystery.

And as we learn more about God and examine the way we live the Christian life, we can choose the changes we would like to make, so as to bring Him pleasure, and a greater peace to ourselves. We may also come to understand with greater confidence that God is faithful to His promises, that Jesus, the Good Shepherd, loves and cares for us beyond measure, and that we can talk with God as often as we wish. This outcome is the work of the Holy Spirit alone.

Bible verses introduce each topic, followed by a commentary that aims to inform, encourage and teach. A section headed 'Thoughts for reflection before we talk with God' is next, where we are invited to mull over various questions raised or statements made, relating to God or aspects of the Christian life, which may be touched upon by the Spirit in our conversation later. Then we have the 'conversation', when we are prompted to imagine a setting in which to meet Jesus and to talk with Him (except chapter 1[9]). The Holy Spirit will take the lead, possibly helping us to hear Jesus first so we can respond, or waiting with us while He, the Spirit, puts the right words in our hearts and minds so we speak first. Once the talking is over, the chapter ends with 'A prayer to finish'.

Conversations may be short, or perhaps around twenty minutes, but they can take longer, sometimes even days; and we can have as many conversations from each chapter as we wish. There is no need to try to remember any of the thoughts we may have had earlier, because the Holy Spirit is leading, and He will bring to mind anything relevant and will guide the conversation to move in the direction He chooses.

For each conversation, we may find it beneficial to have a notebook or a journal handy, so we can jot down the things we wish to remember for the future.

There is help provided for two aspects of the book that may not be familiar to all readers. First, to have a conversation, we need a basic knowledge of how to listen to God, so for those who would like more information on

---

[9] In chapter 1, our conversation is with Father God, and we meet Jesus in all the following chapters,

this subject, a brief guide 'Listening to God' is included below. Second, the conversations rely on us using our imagination, another of God's gifts. The beauty of using imagination in prayer is that we can project our physical senses into the spiritual arena and use them in the way we do in ordinary life. We can see, hear, touch, smell and taste in our thoughts as we imagine biblical events happening, or conversations taking place, adding interest and depth to our interaction with Jesus and Father. For information and suggestions about this, a brief note headed 'Imagining our conversation' is also included below.

Will you take a risk with God and have a conversation? He will be wanting our full attention, but He will meet us any time we choose. If we ask the Holy Spirit where to start, He will answer us – and the first conversation will have started.

Be blessed as you talk with God.

Listening to God

When we have a conversation with God, He will speak to us through the Holy Spirit. God always speaks in love and kindness, so if we hear anything that is not totally infused with love and kindness, it is not God speaking. Some people actually hear God's voice, or hear Him in their imagination; Jesus says 'his sheep follow him because they know his voice',[10] so if that is you, He will be talking gently, maybe in a whisper, and His words are likely to become etched in your memory.

If we do not hear His voice (and that is likely to be most of us), He will speak to us without sound, using a number

---

[10] John 10:4.

of different ways. Here are some of the methods God may use to speak to us:

1. He may speak through a verse in the Bible. If we find our thoughts turning to the Bible and we feel a tug to turn to a particular book, we follow that tug. When we get there, we wait for the Spirit to indicate a chapter to look at. We may need patience to start with, but we can learn how to hear the Spirit by spending time with Him and being alert for His gentle instructions. Then we read the chapter and see which verse or words make an impression on our mind. The Spirit will direct us to His message if we work with Him in humility, patience and perseverance. The Spirit will make us aware of the verse or words He has chosen for us to read and they will have relevance to our prayer, or our question, or the subject we are dealing with.

2. He may give to our mind's eye a picture of an object, an event, a place, a memory or something else relevant to what we are discussing with Him. Often the meaning will be obvious, but at other times we will need to wait for an explanation of what the picture means. The Spirit will explain if we wait for Him patiently. A picture may also be used to give us a Bible verse or a Bible reference, which we can then look up.

3. God may give us a sudden thought, as a result of which we may find we can suddenly understand something that was not understood immediately beforehand. Or we may get a sudden picture that

bears little or no connection to what we were thinking about immediately beforehand; both of these may be revelations from the Holy Spirit. If we are praying for knowledge and understanding about a particular subject and God answers our prayer, He will make it clear which question or subject the answer relates to. God might use sudden thoughts out of nowhere quite often, but we have to be alert to the possibility of this, so that we do not let a sudden thought pass without questioning whether it's from God.

4. He may reveal things to us in other ways – He is God and He can choose as He will. If we have been praying continuously for the answer to a particular question, which is pressing and immediate, we should be expectant that God will talk to us – He does not tease us, He wants to help us. Sometimes a response may take days to come, so that's how long a conversation may last, but don't be discouraged. God hears us and will respond in His time; He knows the whole situation, we seldom do.

Sometimes we do misinterpret what we hear and get it wrong, but this is a learning process. God will talk to any and all people who approach Him to have a conversation, and the more we practise, the better we become. When we hear from God, some answers will be confirmation for what we are thinking already, and some will be revelations that we can trust are from God, because they bring benefit and blessing to us or to others. However, if we believe we have heard God instructing us to take some action, or to discontinue some action, we need to test what we have heard before we rely on it. The safest rule to use is to get a second opinion; so before taking action, or discontinuing some action, we need to ask for corroborating godly advice from a person we trust (or more than one person) who is experienced in listening to God. The Bible contains clear teaching about this:

> Dear friends, do not believe every spirit, but test the spirits to see whether they are from God, because many false prophets have gone out into the world. This is how you can recognise the Spirit of God: every spirit that acknowledges that Jesus Christ has come in the flesh is from God, but every spirit that does not acknowledge Jesus is not from God.[11]

This guidance is a short tutorial about listening to God. There are more ways to hear from God than are mentioned here, and many good books have been written on the subject, so if we wish to know more, we need to ask the Spirit and He will help us find the appropriate title. However, this guidance will be enough to enable any of us to have a conversation with God if, trusting in the power of the Holy Spirit, we will start a conversation, expecting to hear God speak to us in return.

Imagining our conversation

Imagination is from God, and is fun to use. Some readers may not have used imagination in prayer before, so this brief note is to set the scene.

Imagination in prayer is not new, as meditation and contemplation have been used by the Church for

---

[11] 1 John 4:1-3.

centuries. *Lectio Divina*[12] is a method of studying Scripture, with four stages comprising reading, meditation, prayer and contemplation. Ignatian exercises[13] were started in the sixteenth century to help believers discern the will of God for themselves when facing life's big decisions, and they too envisage imagining personal interactions with God in scriptural events. While readers can use these spiritual practices with the quoted scriptures if they wish, the book does not depend on their use for the conversations, since the verses heading each chapter can be read and understood in their everyday meaning; and we will use our imagination to provide the setting for our meetings with God. It is the direct involvement of the Holy Spirit in leading our conversation that ensures the integrity of the exchange.

Anyone can imagine a beautiful and happy scene, and we all do this in our daily lives, without even being aware of it sometimes. However, imagination can produce quite the opposite of a good thing if used without God's protection, when we might imagine harmful, unpleasant or frightening images unintentionally. To avoid this, the conversations are Christ-centred, but also we can defend ourselves by following Paul's example and, 'take captive

---

[12] *Lectio Divina* (meaning Divine Reading) was initiated by St Benedict in the sixth century when he included Scripture reading in his Rule for living, and the process has been refined over the years. For a brief introduction, see www.worthabbey.net/monastic-life/bible-reading (accessed 30th August 2022).
[13] Spiritual exercises were designed by St Ignatius, a Jesuit priest, as a means of helping his followers deepen their prayer life and increase their knowledge of God. See www.iscglasgow.co.uk for information about Ignatian Spirituality (accessed 30th August 2022).

every thought to make it obedient to Christ'.[14] The Holy Spirit will help us in this if we ask Him.

All chapters suggest a setting in which we can imagine where our conversation with Jesus takes place. Most of the stories also suggest how we can imagine our involvement in scenes that form part of Bible events. It is perhaps easier to imagine the surroundings when the event takes place in the open air – there will be more happening – but a closed space still has its attraction because the meeting is likely to be more personal. When we imagine a Bible scene, or the setting for a conversation when we will speak with Jesus, it is helpful to consider the following suggestions.

When we're in the open air, imagine the kerfuffle about Jesus as He walks among the crowds; or if He's with friends, how are the dynamics different? Imagine what happens when He stops, who He speaks to; which friends accompany Him? Imagine what other bystanders near us are saying, and what we can overhear. What about the noise, the smell, the weather? Think about the trees and flowers in the area; the type of ground; what might be happening while the people we are interested in are out of our sight? Perhaps also imagine studying Jesus closely; what does He look like, or sound like? Do His friends stay near to Him or keep their distance? You could examine His eyes, His mannerisms, His demeanour, what He's wearing, and anything else that stands out. Many settings for conversations have us sitting down with Him, but we could imagine Him asking us to go for a walk, or Him leaning against a wall, or over a gate and looking towards the distance, or doing something else. Whatever we

---

[14] 2 Corinthians 10:5.

24

imagine happening can bring the stories off the page and imbue them with life.

If we're inside a room, imagine the background where we're meeting: what's hanging on the walls? Are there windows, curtains, lamps? What's the furniture? If a specific place is suggested, such as a library or a classroom, choose one from your own experience which has good memories. If you can't visualise the suggested place, perhaps find a photo to help: for example, what a wasteland looks like. All these extra details can enhance our experience, and some aspects of the background may be a part of the revelation.

When we imagine Jesus on earth, keep in mind He was a Jewish man who lived a modest life in first-century Palestine; yet He can also be a man of today in our twenty-first-century world. And when we meet with Him, imagine we're spending time with a best friend.

In all this, we need to be led by the Holy Spirit, who may use our imagined pictures to reveal to us wisdom and understanding.

And if minded to do so, we could write the interesting things (words, pictures, verses, sudden thoughts) from our experience in our journal or notebook, as it may help us when we pray over the memory of our meeting, or revisit the scene to continue, or recommence, the conversation with Jesus.

Part One
God and Beginnings

1. The Sky at Night – The beginning of relationship with God

2. The Planets – The beginning of questions addressed to God

3. Creation – The beginning of life on earth

4. Calling and Commissioning – The beginning of service with God

5. The Throne in Heaven – The beginning of the next life

1
The Sky at Night

'To whom will you compare me?
Or who is my equal?' says the Holy One.
Lift up your eyes and look to the heavens:
who created all these?
He who brings out the starry host one by one
and calls forth each of them by name.
Because of his great power and mighty strength,
not one of them is missing ...
Do you not know?
Have you not heard?
The LORD is the everlasting God,
the Creator of the ends of the earth.
He will not grow tired or weary,
and his understanding no one can fathom.[15]

Do you look at the sky at night? It is the most majestic display of light and movement. Some stars are very bright; there are groups of stars that are instantly recognisable; there are those that twinkle and those that do not. We can follow them over the weeks and months as the earth moves in its orbit around the sun and they change their positions relative to where we are standing. They are so

---

[15] Isaiah 40:25-26,28.

big and there are so many – where does humanity fit into all this? Should we stand on the surface of the earth and ask no questions about how they come to be there? Many people do that. Instead of researching the subject, they rely on what other people say – that we are a cosmic accident, and that life will end when we die on earth, and then we will revert to the dust from which we came. But there are many others who do ask questions, who find their faith in a God of love and who read the Bible to discover truth about Him. So Part One is called 'God and Beginnings', when we can consider what God says about Himself; we can think about the origins of what we can see, in space and on the earth, and read how God made us. We can wonder why He talks with us, and can read about the future He offers to those who desire Him.

Believing in God rests on us having a personal relationship with Him, and conversations build relationships. Once the relationship exists, God seeks to deepen it with our cooperation. Believers learn that knowledge and understanding are revealed by God and that humanity could not have progressed so much over the centuries without His assistance. God invites every living soul to have a one-to-one relationship with Him.

Is He a God of love who watches over His creation and cares for His people? Or is He a God of judgement, who makes rules and punishes people when they disobey? Some of us are unsure about who God is, or what He's like, or if creation is His work or something else. Wherever we are in relation to faith, we could start to form perspective by considering the magnitude of the universe, and then consider in turn the sizes of other heavenly bodies within it, until we can appreciate how small we are within the expanse of creation.

Thoughts for reflection before we talk with God

Imagine standing in an open space under the night sky, wondering how you can have a conversation with God about what the people on earth can see in the night sky. Most conversations start with a question. We could ask God about the design of the stars in the sky: their brightness, their size, their position; why some are close together and some are solitary; why some die in our lifetime and not others; why He named them as He did.[16] If 'not one of them is missing',[17] how does He know? When we ask questions, we can say them in our head or speak them aloud, and God will respect us with a reply.

Imagine God in the heavens. What do we think He looks like? How does He travel through His creation? Picture God as He 'lays the foundations of the earth';[18] what might they consist of? Then think about the people living on earth. The Bible has God talking to us as a father talks to his children. Why would He do that if we were not important?

It is no waste of time or effort to be curious about God, or to investigate who He is, for this might produce the treasure that changes our life. We could ask Him why we are here and why He cares for us. Even if we believe already, it is helpful to revisit our long-held beliefs and

---

[16] See Psalm 147:4.

[17] Isaiah 40:26.

[18] Isaiah 51:13.

31

talk with God about them. If there are any misconceptions, it allows opportunity for Him to correct them.

Some people do deny God exists, but then, what is the alternative? That there is no Creator and the world just happened? Is it likely that chance could cause the order and the precision involved in the night sky? Is it believable that an accident could produce the stars and keep them in their positions on the celestial sphere? Why don't we start to talk with God and ask Him about these things and see if He will answer us? He has invited us to talk with Him, so we can expect Him to reveal Himself.

The opening passage from Isaiah instructs us to lift our eyes and 'look to the heavens' as a means of learning about God. It declares, 'the LORD is the everlasting God, the Creator of the ends of the earth.' Why should we trust what the Bible says? Because the scholars of the world over many ages have confirmed that the books of the Old Testament and the New Testament are historical documents of record that can be relied upon for the tenets of the Jewish and Christian faiths. Those who don't believe in God may not have reached a conclusion about the Bible or its origins, but for believers and those seeking God, the Bible is our first port of call. If we ask the Holy Spirit to reveal the truth, He will answer us and tell us what we need to know.

It is time well spent contemplating the night sky. We can talk to God about the lives of people over the past thousands of years, about the world in which they lived and about things that have changed. Yet, by contrast, the stars in the night sky don't seem to have changed at all.

When you have a conversation with God, He will speak through the Holy Spirit. It's important to be still and quiet.

God sometimes whispers,[19] and we may need to practise getting attuned to His voice, but He does want to talk to us, so perseverance will pay a dividend.

The conversation

Imagine looking up at the night sky, God standing beside you in your open space. If you would like the Holy Spirit to speak first, be still and be alert for one of the ways God speaks; alternatively, if you would prefer to start the conversation about how you and God can develop a new, or deepen an existing, personal relationship, wait for the Spirit to bring to your mind some words that you can say, and then be open to the Spirit as the conversation gets going.

A prayer to finish

Creator God, Maker of heaven and earth, Your creation is so big that it makes me realise how small I am. If I avoid thinking about my existence and why I am here, I can live in my own small world. But when I read about Your great power, that You have authority over the stars, and I stop to consider the beauty of creation around me, I see I am part of something much bigger than my present understanding explains.

---

[19] 1 Kings 19:12.

God, please open my mind and heart to receive a new understanding of You as my Maker, and of my relevance in Your world, as I seek to know You better. Amen.

2
The Planets

The heavens declare the glory of God;
the skies proclaim the work of his hands.
Day after day they pour forth speech;
night after night they reveal knowledge.
They have no speech, they use no words;
no sound is heard from them.
Yet their voice goes out into all the earth,
their words to the ends of the world.
In the heavens God has pitched a tent for the sun.
It is like a bridegroom coming out of his chamber,
like a champion rejoicing to run his course.
It rises at one end of the heavens
and makes its circuit to the other;
nothing is deprived of its warmth.[20]

Have you seen the photograph of the earth from space
called the 'Blue Marble'?[21] It was taken by the crew of
Apollo 17 in 1972 and shows our home planet. Compared
with other planets in our solar system, the earth is very
brightly coloured, but all the planets display a staggering
beauty about them. Earth is the only planet with liquid

---

[20] Psalm 19:1-6.
[21] To see a copy of the photograph, search the internet for 'Blue Marble 1972'.

water on its surface, and this makes life possible, enabling people, animals and plants to live. Earth also has oxygen, which living things need to breathe, and the range of the temperature is conducive to life. The sun is the source of light and heat for all the planets and they orbit around it. All the planets spin on an axis; when the earth spins, we get daylight when we face the sun and night when we don't.

How amazing is all this? Expeditions to find life like ours elsewhere in the solar system have produced no evidence, and the likelihood of discovering life elsewhere in the universe seems remote owing to the enormous distances involved, so we have a choice: shall we accept our existence on earth as a bit of good fortune and move on with our busy lives, or shall we search for a credible explanation for our unique existence?

Our quest could start by us asking if God is involved in this. Believers would say most certainly. Although humans have made discoveries about the earth, the solar system and the universe beyond for years, each discovery has tended to show how little we really know. But if God has made us and the heavens reflect His glory, as the above verses declare, then we can expect Him to give us knowledge and understanding, so that we can come to realise knowledge is a gift from God. For the earth is unique, not only for its ability to sustain life, but also because God made humanity 'in his own image'[22] and put us in charge of the earth. So we are God's most precious jewel, and He has given us a wonderful place to live.

---

[22] Genesis 1:27.

And if the earth is amazing, what about the other planets in our solar system – how do they fit in the picture? Our solar system is a part of the heavens, so the planets also declare His glory. Each day they speak to us and reveal knowledge, but without speech, words or sound – right around the world. They are different sizes, beautiful colours, different compositions; some with moons, some without. We have opportunity to study the planets because the knowledge within the world allows us to explore space, as has been evidenced by people landing on the moon, by the International Space Station, by sending the expeditions that landed vehicles on Mars, and the spacecrafts that have travelled to Saturn and beyond.

The spiritual reasons for the earth are considered later in the book, but what of the spiritual significance of the planets? Can we discern from God the spiritual reasons for their existence? Certainly they give us perspective; our solar system is tiny within the universe, but they are still towards the limit of our reach and capabilities when it comes to visiting any of them physically, and we have yet to discover any reason beyond their scientific purposes in God's plans. Yet God designed, created and positioned them, and made them all different; why is that?

Thoughts for reflection before we talk with God

Imagine you are talking with God about creation. God the Father, God the Son and God the Holy Spirit have all been involved, for God uses His plural address in the creation account.[23] It is good to talk with Jesus about the things of

---

[23] Genesis 1:26.

God because He lived on earth as a man and has experienced already everything we will ever know.

What if Jesus were to ask us about the planets? How would we respond? Do the planets speak to us in some way, perhaps through their different orbits, or atmospheres, sizes or colours? If God has a purpose for the earth, why would He not have a purpose for the other planets too? The solar system is so complex, yet it operates in perfect balance, so everything must have its purpose. Scientists have their theories about the beginning of life on earth, but find no life like ours anywhere else, while the Bible tells us heaven and earth are God's work. If the heavens are no accident, but a God-designed space, what do we think the planets might be used for? Might they be a place, perhaps, where heavenly beings live in the Spirit? Are they different because there is no sin there?

Consider our relationship with God. He is our creator, and He is Spirit, whereas we, His created, are mortal. We shouldn't be surprised we know so little about everything, for He is God, not us, but He does want us to grow in knowledge and understanding: that's why He tells us to lift our eyes to the heavens.

Can you imagine God watching over the universe and the solar system? Some of the photographs obtained during the more recent space missions give us some idea of the size and extent of the heavens.[24] How can this not affect how we picture God – what He looks like, His greatness and power? With so many heavenly bodies visible, we might ask why we belong to this solar system,

---

[24] See, for example, www.nasa.gov/webbfirstimages (accessed 26th August 2022).

and what is special about 'our' planets? How can we know God as 'Maker of heaven and earth'[25] and still relate to Him when He says He wants to talk to us? Perhaps the heavens are used by God to instruct us that we need to enlarge our imagination and expectations of who He is. In the book of Revelation, at the end of time God promises '"a new heaven and a new earth," for the first heaven and the first earth had passed away'.[26] If He can do this, He must be very powerful indeed.

When we compare our smallness with God's indescribable greatness and look at the heavens He created, it must surely ask us to take stock of who He is. God is such a mystery, and we must never think we can contain Him. Despite all the unknowns, we are significant enough in God's plan and purpose that He wants to talk to us as His children. Isn't that astounding?

The conversation

Imagine flying through the solar system in a space ship. You are at the controls and you can go wherever you want to. Jesus is sitting beside you in the co-pilot's seat. It's an amazing experience. As you come near your favourite planet and inspect it closely, let the Holy Spirit lead and prompt you with a question for Jesus which He lays on your heart, about the heavens and how God uses them to declare His glory.

---

[25] Psalm 146:6.
[26] Revelation 21:1.

A prayer to finish

God, I can see the beauty of all You have made and I praise You for it. I am sorry that I listen to the voices of the world sometimes, which can so easily lead me to doubt You, when I could be listening to You.

Lord, I pray, open my mind and heart to recognise Your truth, grant me courage to ask You questions about Yourself and what You've made, and give me grace to believe what You say, that I may understand my place in Your creation, and be glad of it. Amen.

3
Creation

In the beginning God created the heavens and the earth.
Now the earth was formless and empty, darkness was over
the surface of the deep, and the Spirit of God was hovering
over the waters.
And God said, 'Let there be light,' and there was light.[27]

Thus the heavens and the earth were completed in all their
vast array.
By the seventh day God had finished the work he had been
doing; so on the seventh day he rested from all his work.
Then God blessed the seventh day and made it holy,
because on it he rested from all the work of creating that he
had done.[28]

In the beginning was the Word, and the Word was with
God, and the Word was God. He was with God in the
beginning. Through him all things were made; without him
nothing was made that has been made. In him was life, and
that life was the light of all mankind. The light shines in
the darkness, and the darkness has not overcome it.[29]

---

[27] Genesis 1:1-3.

[28] Genesis 2:1-3.

[29] John 1:1-5.

The story of the creation, as written in the book of Genesis, is very well known. It does not give any scientific fact to explain how the world was created, but informs us that the origins of heaven and earth are an act of God. The first chapter records what God said on the first eleven occasions He spoke, while doing His creative work, and that His first instruction was for there to be light, which brought light into the darkness and enabled God's work to be seen. Over the first three days, we are told God separated light from darkness and sea from sky, and gathered the water in one place so that the land could produce vegetation and trees with fruit-bearing seed. On the next three days, God put lights in the sky, made the fish for the sea, birds for the sky and placed animals on the land, ending with the final touch of making men and women in His own image to rule over the earth. Then God blessed the people, told them to be fruitful and said they should 'fill the earth and subdue it'. Thus the emptiness of the earth was filled.[30]

Can we, or should we, believe the Genesis account of the creation? The apostle Paul tells Timothy that 'all Scripture is God-breathed',[31] and the apostle Peter affirms that the people who wrote Scripture 'spoke from God as they were carried along by the Holy Spirit',[32] so it comes down to whether or not we choose to believe it. Genesis is not a scientific account, but an invitation to faith. The Bible states the Holy Spirit was present at the beginning,

---

[30] See Genesis 1:1-31.

[31] 2 Timothy 3:16.

[32] 2 Peter 1:21.

'hovering over the waters',[33] so we can ask Him to help us discern the truth, and help us to believe it.

In the New Testament, the beginning of John's Gospel echoes the opening words of Genesis. John proclaims that Jesus is the Word, that Jesus is God and that through Him everything was made. So this is the creation story being repeated from a different perspective. If we are open to talking with God, the truth will be explained to us.

Thoughts for reflection before we talk with God

Imagine you are an observer at the creation. You are sitting in God's planning office and you picture in your mind what the earth looks like when it is 'formless and empty'. It's dark, so there is not much to see, but the Holy Spirit is present. Then God issues His creative words, the first being, 'Let there be light,' and the picture starts to change. You can see God designing the sky – its composition means that sometimes it's a deep blue, sometimes a light blue with white wispy clouds, sometimes pale yellow and, at times in the morning or at the end of the day, it can have that amazing redness. Can you hear God exclaim how beautiful it is?

Then God is gathering the water and revealing dry land, which becomes covered with plants and trees; He designs the night sky, and the sun and the moon are starting to shine; and He is creating the fish, and the birds, and the animals. There is such variation in scale; compare the sun, the ocean, the elephant and the ant. Think about how tectonic plates work, and the world's weather system, and the gems buried deep in the earth; the different areas

---

[33] Genesis 1:2.

43

of vegetation in the world, like the rainforests and the desert; the beauty of enormous trees, and big flowers, and the most delicate of small flowers. What about the variety of animals and birds across the continents, their different shapes, colours and habits? Or the creatures in the seas, ranging from the biggest of whales to the smallest of fish, the wonderful colours of tropical fish and birds, and the beauty of birdsong?

We are still learning about the deep-sea world, and there are places where humans have never been. In our small way, we too have created things with our hands and made images in our minds that reflect the creative character of our Maker and Creator. This is a consequence of being made in His image.

Bring to your mind some of the things you created as a child, or in your adult life, that relate to the creation story. If you can demonstrate a talent in one of the creative arts, look for where God has used it while He was creating the earth. Whatever talents we may have, God had them first.

Let us celebrate with God the wonder of His creation. It is so complex, so clever, so interesting, so colourful, that we can honour Him by spending time reflecting on aspects of what He has created. His knowledge is beyond our understanding; scientific principles undergird each step of creation, but much of the science is still unknown to humanity.

And after making the heavens and the earth, God made Adam and Eve and gave them the garden to live in. The fall of humankind was later, but at the start, the garden was beautiful and abundant, a safe place to live and to enjoy God's company. As the inhabitants of this amazing world today, with dominion over its resources, we would do well to pay our respects and thank God for His generous provision.

Jesus was in the planning office at the time of creation; imagine you are there and you know you will have the opportunity to talk with Him later about the creation. What might you say? Would you like to ask if the law of the jungle (ie when the strong survives at the expense of the weak) was part of the original design, or a consequence of the Fall? Or if desert areas were intended? Are there fish in the sea that humanity will never discover? Perhaps you would ask if life like ours is elsewhere in the universe. Or why it takes so many years for scientific knowledge to be revealed. Perhaps ask Him if He enjoys sharing His joy of creation with us, in the way we love sharing our joys and happiness with family and friends.

The conversation

Imagine yourself and Jesus walking in the Garden of Eden in the early morning. There are trees with fruit to eat, and many flowers; it's the most beautiful garden you've ever seen. God created all that grows there and Jesus would be knowledgeable, for it was all made 'through him and for him'.[34] Perhaps you might make a remark about something you see in the garden that intrigues you, or if you see your favourite flower or shrub. If you are lost for words, let the Holy Spirit prompt you with some words that He knows you would like to ask about life on earth.

---

[34] Colossians 1:16.

45

A prayer to finish

Lord, thank You that we live in such a beautiful world. You are an amazing designer. You give us authority to manage the world and the opportunity to imitate You in our gardens, hobbies, farming and conservation.

I am sorry we've spoilt so much of it. We seem unable to care for it properly on our own and we desperately need Your guidance. Help us to pray, please, that we will be wise enough to ask You for Your guidance and direction in our decision-making, and humble enough to receive Your truth and apply it. Thank You. Amen.

4
Calling and Commissioning

In the year that King Uzziah died, I saw the Lord, high and
exalted, seated on a throne; and the train of his robe filled
the temple. Above him were seraphim, each with six wings:
with two wings they covered their faces, with two they
covered their feet, and with two they were flying. And they
were calling to one another:
'Holy, holy, holy is the LORD Almighty;
the whole earth is full of his glory.'
At the sound of their voices the doorposts and thresholds
shook and the temple was filled with smoke.
'Woe to me!' I cried. 'I am ruined! For I am a man of
unclean lips, and I live among a people of unclean lips, and
my eyes have seen the King, the LORD Almighty.'
Then one of the seraphim flew to me with a live coal in his
hand, which he had taken with tongs from the altar. With it
he touched my mouth and said, 'See, this has touched your
lips; your guilt is taken away and your sin atoned for.'
Then I heard the voice of the Lord saying, 'Whom shall I
send? And who will go for us?'
And I said, 'Here am I. Send me!'[35]

Prophets, like Isaiah, are people who are called by God to
speak on His behalf when He wishes to communicate with

---

[35] Isaiah 6:1-8.

His people. No one can volunteer to be a prophet and only a small number have been chosen. The Bible books of prophecy are divided between earlier and later prophets, and the latter are divided between major prophets, whose books are lengthy, and minor prophets, whose books are usually quite short. Their words are referred to frequently in the New Testament.

Isaiah was a major prophet in Israel's history and considered by many to be the greatest of all the prophets. The above passage describes his commissioning by God. It has God sitting on His throne, being praised by flying heavenly beings called seraphim, calling to each other, which gives us some idea of God's majesty, holiness and power. The realisation by Isaiah that he has seen God while still a sinful man makes him afraid for his life and he cries out in despair. Fortunately for him, one of the seraphim acts with haste to bring cleansing and forgiveness, and when God asks for someone to take a message to His people, Israel, Isaiah offers himself for service.

The message to Israel was to stop worshipping false gods, or trusting in alliances with neighbours, and to trust in God alone, acting in a way that befitted Israel's status as a 'holy people'.[36] Isaiah duly delivered the message as God instructed him to do, and the book of Isaiah contains this message; but it also tells of judgement to come, and gives the first news of a child to be born, who will come to save the world.[37]

---

[36] Exodus 22:31.
[37] See Isaiah 9:6; Isaiah 53.

God still calls to His service, and commissions, those who believe in Him. For many people, their calling or commissioning is a memorable event, as it proved for Isaiah, who wrote down what happened to him. In Old Testament times, some big characters had major tasks given to them, such as Isaiah himself; or Moses, who led the people of Israel out of slavery in Egypt; or Joshua, who led the people into the promised land of Canaan; or Jeremiah, called to be a prophet. In New Testament times, the first disciples, Peter and Andrew, and James and John were called by Jesus to leave their fishing boats and follow Him, which they did without any delay.[38] Many other people were given lesser tasks to carry out over the years, but the Bible is filled with all kinds of personalities who were called by God to lead, to prophesy[39] or to perform some particular task that He required. The same happens to believers today.

Every calling is unique and every given task is treasured in the kingdom of God. It can be done only by the person called to do it. Once we surrender to God and agree to follow Him in obedience and humility, calling becomes our way of life. Commissioning is when we are appointed within our calling to carry out a particular role or task. God always equips those He calls for their tasks, and thus we are never expected to do God's work in our own strength, or without the training and help of His

---

[38] See Mark 1:16-20.

[39] Prophets like Isaiah are called by God to speak to His people and are few in number. However, there are spiritual gifts which were given to the early Church, one of which is the gift of prophecy, and these are still given today. More information can be found in Romans 12:6-8; 1 Corinthians 12:8-11; Ephesians 4:11.

guiding Spirit. We also benefit from God's grace, by which we mean His totally undeserved favour, and this is always available and sufficient for our needs.[40]

Thoughts for reflection before we talk with God

Visualise yourself going with Isaiah to the throne room and seeing and hearing what Isaiah is describing – the movement of the seraphim with their six wings, and their voices; can you imagine the doorposts shaking, or the smell of the smoke? What would be your reaction? As God is not limited by time, this worship could be happening even as you read this.

Has there been a time in your life when you have felt overawed by your surroundings? Did you sense the presence of God with you then? Does Isaiah's description of God on His throne help you to appreciate the majesty and glory of God?

It would be hard to find an equivalent scene on earth, yet God is taking the trouble to inform us about this; why might that be? Is it to challenge our pride or, perhaps, our apathy? Maybe it's to help us realise what a serious business it is having such a powerful God as our Creator, Saviour and 'Advocate'.[41]

Every disciple of Jesus is called to serve in the kingdom of God. Do you remember the moment when you decided to follow Jesus? Not everyone does, and sometimes we grow into our calling over time. Jesus gave every believer the Great Commission, which is to 'make disciples of all nations, baptising them in the name of the Father and of

---

[40] See 2 Corinthians 12:9.
[41] John 14:26.

the Son and of the Holy Spirit, and teaching them to obey everything' that He had spoken. He also said, 'I am with you always, to the very end of the age,'[42] so we don't do this on our own.

Perhaps there's been a time when someone has asked you about your beliefs and you shared your story, or you felt prompted to talk to someone else about faith? This could be the Holy Spirit working in you and through you.

If you sense you want to say, or say again, some words of commitment, you can say them any time. God will hear you and bless you for answering His call. If you're unsure what to say, trust the Holy Spirit to help you. We don't need formal words, and He is always listening. The words you say will include a plea for Jesus to become the Lord of your life and your future. If you meet Jesus and talk with Him, you could ask Him for faith, or courage, or understanding, or all of them and more; if you have a heart for a particular role in life, perhaps a teaching role, or overseas work, or maybe ordination or lay ministry, you could ask Him about that. Having a conversation with Jesus has no limits, so let the Holy Spirit guide you on what you discuss.

The conversation

Imagine meeting Jesus outside your home as you return from shopping, or as you take in a parcel delivery. He meets people in everyday places, as He did with the fishermen. He chooses a quiet place for you to sit together, and He invites you to speak first; is there an aspect of calling or commissioning relating to your own experience

---

[42] Matthew 28:19-20.

that you wish to talk to Him about? Or if you prefer, let the Spirit take the lead and listen for Jesus to speak to you.

A prayer to finish

Lord, thank You that You have called me to know You. I do want to follow You, and to learn as we journey together. Whatever You ask of me, I will trust You, because I am confident I will be equipped with everything I need. By Your Spirit, grant me contentment and courage as we travel, and may I share Your grace with those I meet on the way. Thank You. Amen.

5

The Throne in Heaven

*After this I looked, and there before me was a door standing
open in heaven. And the voice I had first heard speaking to
me like a trumpet said, 'Come up here, and I will show you
what must take place after this.' At once I was in the Spirit,
and there before me was a throne in heaven with someone
sitting on it. And the one who sat there had the appearance
of jasper and ruby. A rainbow that shone like an emerald
encircled the throne. Surrounding the throne were twenty-
four other thrones, and seated on them were twenty-four
elders. They were dressed in white and had crowns of gold
on their heads. From the throne came flashes of lightning,
rumblings and peals of thunder. In front of the throne,
seven lamps were blazing. These are the seven spirits of
God. Also in front of the throne there was what looked like
a sea of glass, clear as crystal.
In the centre, round the throne, were four living creatures,
and they were covered with eyes, in front and behind.*[43]

In the book of Revelation, the apostle John writes from his
exile on the island of Patmos, to pass on the revelation of
Jesus concerning the future of the world. The book opens
with various greetings from John, then has letters to seven
churches on earth, and then a vision of future events. The

---

[43] Revelation 4:1-6.

book tells of the victory Jesus has achieved over death and the future life that believers in Him will share with Him, so He encourages us to stand firm against compromise with the world, and persecution, until He comes again, when He will gather His followers and the world will be judged.

It was the Roman Empire that dominated when John was writing about compromise, but while the identity of the worldly powers may be different today, compromise and persecution remain a danger, so the message for us to stand firm is still relevant. Life and death on earth is not the end; we look forward to life after death too.

John's description of the throne room in heaven is the beginning of his vision and adds to the picture given in Isaiah 6:1-8.[44] John is called to the throne room, in the way Moses was called to Mount Sinai to receive the Ten Commandments, which God wrote on two stone tablets.[45] The scene that greets John is one of the brightest splendour and gives a foretaste of what God promises to believers. God lives in light of unapproachable brilliance and is attended by twenty-four elders, and four living creatures who are described as having six wings and being 'covered with eyes all round'.[46] With all the light and sound, it must be overwhelming. Would we ever have imagined this if we hadn't been told?

It is helpful to have a picture in our mind of where we're going when we travel, and the journey of life on earth is no exception. God wants His family to know that

---

[44] See chapter 4.

[45] See Exodus 31:18.

[46] 1 Timothy 6:16; Revelation 4:8.

the end of life here involves reaching a real place with real people elsewhere. John's record of his vision is a gift to inspire us about our future. God promises His people life without end, with God Himself living among us. He will be our God and we will be His people. He will wipe away all our tears, and death, mourning, crying and pain will be things of the past, for the old things will have been replaced by a new creation.[47]

The life we are living on earth today does have death, grief, tears and pain. Jesus warned us when He walked the earth that we will have trouble, but that we shouldn't be despondent about it, because He has 'overcome the world'.[48] He also said that heaven is a spacious place and, after His ascension into heaven, He will return to earth at the right time to collect us; then all of us will live together with Him in heaven.[49]

This is a wonderful reassurance about the life that is waiting for believers in the future, but we have to continue standing firm in our faith today, as the first-century believers had to do in their times.

Thoughts for reflection before we talk with God

Imagine you are with the apostle John in his vision. You have been invited into the throne room so that God can show you where He lives and who lives there with Him. Jesus has promised we will live there too. You can see God on His throne in the middle of the amazing light show, with rumblings and thunder.

---

[47] See Revelation 21:3-4.
[48] John 16:33.
[49] See John 14:2-3.

What are your first impressions on seeing God and the others in this setting? We tend not to think about this much, but perhaps we should. If we follow Jesus, this is our destination. You can see the twenty-four elders sitting on their thrones around God. The four creatures are also visible, forever saying how holy is the Lord, and that He is eternal.[50] When the living creatures worship Him who sits on the throne, the elders on the twenty-four thrones fall down, worship Him, lay down their crowns and say that God is worthy 'to receive glory and honour and power', because He created everything.[51] This extravagant worship is rarely, if ever, found on earth.

All the words spoken by the twenty-four elders and the living creatures are words of worship, fitting for God Himself. Our words also carry great power, for we are made in God's image, and His words created the earth and the heavens. How careful we should be that our words are appropriate as we make our journey towards heaven.

When we compare this description of the throne room in heaven with our knowledge of earth, we might well ask how we fit into this heavenly kingdom when it's all so different, when we are so small and so fragile? There seems such a mismatch between the inhabitants in heaven and us, mere mortals, on earth. Yet God has made a way, and the answer is that once we believe in Jesus, He lives in us and we in Him. He takes on the responsibility for our admission into heaven and He clothes us with His

---

[50] See Revelation 4:8.
[51] See Revelation 4:9-11.

'righteousness' and His 'holiness'.[52] No one else can do this for us.

To meet God in His throne room requires our complete surrender of self. Sometimes the only acceptable response to God is to be silent, as the prophet Habakkuk learned in a conversation with God.[53] Perhaps think about what you might ask Jesus when you speak to Him, as He sits at God's right hand.

Do you have questions about heaven? It may stretch our imagination even to think of ourselves in such a place. Do we wonder if all heavenly beings speak the same language in heaven? How do we move about in heaven? How soon will we meet God face to face once the new creation starts? When will we meet our loved ones who have gone before us? There is so much we can be curious about.

The conversation

You're still in the throne room; imagine now being invited to speak with Jesus, seated in His place in heaven. You sit on a seat near Him. In such a situation, you might be feeling a little overawed, but the Holy Spirit lives here too and imparts His peace to you. Will you wait on the Spirit to lead you into a conversation about what life eternal with Jesus might be like, while living beside 'the river of the water of life'?[54]

---

[52] 1 Corinthians 1:30.
[53] See Habakkuk 2:20.
[54] Revelation 22:1.

A prayer to finish

We praise You, Lord God, from everlasting to everlasting. Greatness, power, glory, majesty and splendour all belong to You, for everything in heaven and earth is Yours already. Yours also is the kingdom and You are the head over everything. All honour and wealth come from You and You are the ruler of everything. Strength is in Your hands, and the power to exalt. You give strength to us.[55]

Thank You, Lord, for the picture of Your throne room, and our journey's end. May I keep my eyes fixed on my Saviour, Jesus, until I get there. Amen.

---

[55] Based on 1 Chronicles 29:10-12.

Part Two
What is God Like?

6. Jesus Feeds the Five Thousand – God is generous

7. Peter Walks on Water – God is trustworthy

8. Child of God – God loves us unconditionally

9. If You're Willing – He is the God who heals us

10. Fearfully and Wonderfully Made – God is divine and human

11. Father, Forgive Them – Jesus forgives to show us we can too

12. Mary – God loves us for who we are, our significance rests in Him

13. Jesus is the Only Way – God's way to salvation

14. The Supremacy of Christ – God affirms all authority belongs to Jesus

15. Greater Love Has No One – God loves us beyond our imagination

6
Jesus Feeds the Five Thousand

As evening approached, the disciples came to him and said,
'This is a remote place, and it's already getting late. Send
the crowds away, so that they can go to the villages and
buy themselves some food.'
Jesus replied, 'They do not need to go away. You give them
something to eat.'
'We have here only five loaves of bread and two fish,' they
answered.
'Bring them here to me,' he said. And he told the people to
sit down on the grass. Taking the five loaves and the two
fish and looking up to heaven, he gave thanks and broke the
loaves. Then he gave them to the disciples, and the disciples
gave them to the people. They all ate and were satisfied, and
the disciples picked up twelve basketfuls of broken pieces
that were left over. The number of those who ate was about
five thousand men, besides women and children.[56]

This story tells us about the compassion and generosity of
God. Jesus had just heard about the fate of His cousin John
the Baptist, so He and His disciples had sailed by boat to
a remote spot to spend some time on their own. But once
the crowd learned about this, they walked along the shore
to where the boat was heading, so when the boat landed,

---

[56] Matthew 14:15-21.

instead of resting, Jesus took pity on the people and healed those who were sick. By evening, because of the remote location, the disciples were worried about the people's welfare, since only some of them had brought food. The disciples' solution was to send the people away to fend for themselves, but Jesus thought differently. He said they didn't need to leave and told the disciples to 'give them something to eat'. The challenge Jesus gave His disciples would probably have silenced most people, but to give them credit, the disciples did have the courage to say they had found someone with five loaves and two fish. Perhaps they also questioned silently under their breath how far that would go for such a large crowd.

To God, a small amount of anything good we have has significant value, even if we have our doubts. Jesus told the disciples to bring Him the food they had obtained and then He showed what can be achieved when He becomes involved. Jesus told the people to sit down – which we could interpret as Him saying, 'Leave it with Me, I can do this, all will be well, trust Me.' Once the people obeyed, the power of God could take over. Looking towards heaven, Jesus gave thanks to His Father, broke the loaves and had the food distributed. So all the people 'ate and were satisfied', and the disciples picked up the leftover pieces, each collecting a basketful.

In providing so much food, Jesus shows His desire to give His people more than they will need. He was generous too with the wine at Cana[57] and with the feeding of the four thousand.[58] This aspect of His character can be

---

[57] See John 2:6-10.
[58] See Mark 8:6-8.

seen again and again if we bring Jesus our little amount of faith, our feeble courage, our good intentions, or any other offering that seems insufficient for the moment. Jesus does not hold back, but responds by making up the shortfall with generosity and grace.

Thoughts for reflection before we talk with God

Imagine you are in the crowd that day. You have come with the rest of your family or a group of friends, and you're all glad to be there because you have learned so much from the new teacher – but none of you expected to stay so long, so you haven't brought enough to eat. Now Grandpa is becoming tired and listless from lack of food, the children are hungry and getting fractious, your siblings, wife or husband, friends, they're all getting tetchy. Or perhaps you came alone and never gave food a thought. What do you do?

Imagine looking towards the front of the crowd and wondering what to do; you can see the teacher and His friends in a huddle and they're talking; then you see the crowd in front of you starting to sit down in groups. What is happening? You hear there is food being provided. Where's that come from? There must be thousands of people here today. The teacher's friends are handing it out. Imagine the relief and the excitement as the friends get nearer. You're hoping they don't run out before you receive some; then you receive your portion and it's the best food you have ever tasted. Later, you hear that everyone was fed and there were lots of leftovers, which were all collected.

Has there been in your own experience an occasion when you were excited by something that caught your attention and you rushed in to be part of it, only to find later that the lack of planning created difficulties? You felt angry with yourself because you knew you could have done better. So how did it turn out? Was there a good result? Looking back, can you see the hand of God in this?

Visualise the scene at the end of the meal; you want to meet Jesus and He is walking through the crowd. There are many people trying to catch His attention, but Jesus sees you and moves in your direction. As He comes near, what is your first impression? Does He give you a sense of calm, or does He make you feel unsure of yourself? You followed Him to this remote place because you wanted to experience something of His presence. How does it feel now you are standing next to Him? Can you describe it?

Jesus has done something impossible, yet no one saw Him do anything, except pray to God. What did He say? There would surely be a 'thank you' to God, but might He tell us more of what has just occurred?

On this day by the lake, Jesus received from the crowd what food they could offer, and returned to them more food than they could eat. He showed them He loved them by meeting their need without delay. He repeated the miracle when He fed the four thousand.

How many times do we pray in a panic, or in an emergency, for immediate help, and then God shows His love to us when He intervenes in our lives and saves the situation? He wants us to trust Him in this. If we act with a sincere heart, it seems the less we have to give to Jesus, the more He gives back to us to help with what we need, and in quick time.

To have a conversation with Jesus about His converting our small offerings into His abundant gifts would be faith-building. You may like to mention this when you have your conversation.

The conversation

Now you and Jesus have moved a little distance away from the people around you, and you are both sitting on the grass. It's getting dark, but someone has a lantern nearby. Do you want to mention a time you remember clearly because God was so generous to you? Or will you enjoy the contentment you feel from just sitting in His presence, and let the Spirit use a memory or a word to open the conversation about the goodness and abundance of God?

A prayer to finish

Thank You, Lord, that in the times when I rushed ahead without proper thought, or my impetuousness landed me in a difficult situation, You were there to rescue me and bring me to a place of safety.

Thank You for Your generosity, that You give me more than I need or ask for. Please let me be alert to Your involvement in my life all the time, not just when I'm in trouble and asking for help; and grant me a good heart, please, that I can be truly grateful. Amen.

7
Peter Walks on Water

*Shortly before dawn Jesus went out to them, walking on the
lake. When the disciples saw him walking on the lake, they
were terrified. 'It's a ghost,' they said, and cried out in fear.
But Jesus immediately said to them: 'Take courage! It is I.
Don't be afraid.'
'Lord, if it's you,' Peter replied, 'tell me to come to you on
the water.'
'Come,' he said.
Then Peter got down out of the boat, walked on the water
and came towards Jesus. But when he saw the wind, he was
afraid and, beginning to sink, cried out, 'Lord, save me!'
Immediately Jesus reached out his hand and caught him.
'You of little faith,' he said, 'why did you doubt?'
And when they climbed into the boat, the wind died
down.*[59]

In this story, Peter was at his impetuous best. Changing
from being terrified to trusting in a moment, he said to
Jesus, 'Lord, if it's you ... tell me to come to you on the
water.' His heart was all for Jesus – he had no doubts in
that moment. And the Gospel records he did actually walk
on the water. It was when Peter looked at the wind that

---

[59] Matthew 14:25-32.

his faith receded, the terror reasserted itself and he began to sink. Peter prayed what people down the centuries have prayed in times of extreme fear: 'Lord, save me!'

Jesus didn't refuse Peter's request to walk with Him on the water; He encouraged him to step out in faith, and Peter succeeded while he looked at Jesus. It was only when he changed his focus to the wind that he started to sink. Yet Jesus was there, ready to reach out His hand as soon as it was necessary.

We should be understanding towards Peter. Verse 24 of this passage reports the boat was 'buffeted by the waves because the wind was against it'. In the middle of the sea, in a high wind, it takes courage to step out. Peter was a fisherman and he would know a dangerous sea when he saw it. Yes, Jesus was with him, but the strength of the wind still captured his focus.

Often we can fall into the same mindset and look at 'the wind' blowing against us, when our safety is with Jesus. He may have chided Peter for his lack of faith, but it was gently done and said with love. Jesus wants all His followers to take risks, to trust Him and try walking with Him on the water, so He is not angry if we fail. He knows we may lose our courage or our strength and start to sink, but He is always close by, ready to reach out and help us in our moment of need, and to use the experience to teach us how to succeed next time.

Thoughts for reflection before we talk with God

Imagine you and Jesus together in the boat. You are enjoying the time spent in company with Him and the small band of disciples. Your heart's desire is to please

Him, to know Him better, to earn His commendation and be a winning team together. So, what if Jesus steps out of the boat and calls on you to imitate Peter and try walking on the water? In your imagination, you step out and set off towards Jesus, and you succeed, so that you meet up and walk joyfully back to the boat and get on board together. The other disciples are full of laughter and share in the joy of having seen one of their own do an amazing thing with the Lord. What do you think Jesus might have said to you after such derring-do?

Has there been an occasion in your life when you decided to take a risk to serve the Lord? You might have said to yourself, 'It's like walking on the water and I will do this,' and off you went. Perhaps the risk was worthwhile because you succeeded and the work had a wonderful harvest... or perhaps it all went wrong and the plan didn't work; you didn't achieve what you intended because things started to get out of control and you felt you were sinking. Did you cry to the Lord to save you? Did you recover the situation and then, when looking back, find a 'God-coincidence' that significantly helped your efforts?

Peter climbing out of the boat is similar to what we may do if we feel a bit bullish. We trust Jesus to help us in trouble, even if our predicament is dire; and if it gets worse, we keep pressing on, because we think walking on water must have seemed impossible to Peter, until he did it. But a bit later, we can look again at our situation, with less-believing eyes, and see how hopeless it looks now to ourselves and to other people; perhaps we start thinking how naïve we must have been to still believe, when Jesus surely would have acted already, without our asking, if

He was going to help; so we lose hope, and like Peter, we cry out as we begin to sink.

Jesus told the disciples not to be afraid, but Peter was afraid because he looked at his circumstances. We may do this as well, but because He cared for Peter, Jesus saved him, and as He cares for us too, the same compassion is available to us. The wind might be seen as representing the realities of our situation, and the negative assumptions we make about the world which seek to undermine our faith at every opportunity, but once Jesus and Peter were back in the boat, 'the wind died down'. If we stick with Jesus in our storm, the world will retreat from us too.

'Faith is confidence in what we hope for and assurance about what we do not see.'[60] Jesus commended great faith when He found it, like with the centurion,[61] and chided His disciples on several occasions for their 'little faith'.[62] Faith is given by God, and we can ask for more, knowing there is no limit. He wants us to live our lives trusting in Him, relying on our reserves of faith. If we fail to display enough faith, He may challenge us, but He wants us to try again, not staying in the place that relies on our own strength. He told His disciples to believe what they had seen Him do and He challenges us to do this too; the miracles are the evidence that God does take care of all our needs.

What would you like to talk about with Jesus? What about why it's so difficult to keep our faith in times of adversity? Or, considering all His past help and blessing

---

[60] Hebrews 11:1.

[61] See Matthew 8:5-10.

[62] See, for example, Matthew 8:26.

in our lives, why do we sometimes find that our faith disintegrates at the important moment, as it did for Peter? Can we properly keep our eyes fixed on Him when fear invades our thinking and destroys our peace? And how do we recover from the shame that often weighs us down after we fail, or lose faith, and sink? Ask the Spirit to guide your thinking and words as you prepare to talk with Jesus.

The conversation

Imagine yourself with Jesus, still in the boat, sitting apart from the others, talking quietly after the noise of the day has died down. It's calmer now, just a slight breeze, and Jesus is ready to listen. At His invitation to start the conversation, you could ask about how to trust Him more, especially when external factors try to steal our gaze away; or you can look to the Spirit to guide you with a thought or a word that will open up possibilities for growing a deeper, stronger faith.

A prayer to finish

Thank You, Lord, for being my support and my encouragement in life, whatever the stresses of my daily existence. You know I want to serve You and stand up for You, and that my faith can fade if I look at the obstacles or the opposition.

Thank You for keeping faith with me, whatever. I want to take more risks with You, Lord, and I will try to walk on water again.

Increase my trust in You, I pray, that I will be more believing next time. Amen.

8
Child of God

So he got up and went to his father.
But while he was still a long way off, his father saw him
and was filled with compassion for him; he ran to his son,
threw his arms round him and kissed him.
The son said to him, 'Father, I have sinned against heaven
and against you. I am no longer worthy to be called your
son.'
But the father said to his servants, 'Quick! Bring the best
robe and put it on him. Put a ring on his finger and
sandals on his feet. Bring the fattened calf and kill it. Let's
have a feast and celebrate. For this son of mine was dead
and is alive again; he was lost and is found.'[63]

Jesus is telling some parables to illustrate the Father's love, emphasising that there is more joy in heaven over one person who acts contrary to God's law and admits it when they know they're wrong, than any number of others who don't accept the possibility of their being in the wrong, and thus see no need to say they're sorry. He starts with a parable about the good shepherd and the lost sheep, in which He likens God to a shepherd who is prepared to leave ninety-nine sheep in the open country to look for the

---

[63] Luke 15:20-24.

one who has wandered away. Then He tells us about a woman who lost a silver coin, searching intently until she found it, and says God acts likewise, searching for us in dark places and rejoicing when He finds the one who is lost.[64] Lastly, He tells the parable about the lost son, in which He highlights again Father God's unconditional love for His people. In today's language, He might paraphrase the story into something like this:

> The child had decided. Parental oversight was finished, so he demanded his inheritance from his father, while telling him he wished he was dead, and left to follow his own heart. There was no going back; he knew best. Unfortunately, it didn't happen the way it was meant to and the son found the world to be a cruel place. He had lots of friends while he had money and could enjoy living his dream, but once the money ran out, the friends did too. Eventually he ended up begging for scraps in a dead-end job, at which point he came to his senses. He swallowed his pride, practised how he would apologise, and began the long journey home. While still a long way off, he was spotted in the distance by his father, who had not forgotten him, who still loved him, whose aching heart still waited in hope for reconciliation. Without hesitation, the father ran to the son, threw his arms around him and kissed him. The son admitted his wrongs and said he was sorry, which the father accepted, but spent little time dwelling on. Instead, he hurried his servants, and the son was given the best robe, which signified

---

[64] See Luke 15:4-10.

position and acceptance; a ring on his finger, which signified status and authority; and sandals, which made him family again. The child was reinstated into the father's house and a celebration party, with the best food and wine, was given for friends and relatives to celebrate his return.

The story of the child and the father mirrors what happens between the children of God who decide to return home and the heavenly Father who waits for them.

Thoughts for reflection before we talk with God

Was there a time when you decided to follow your own heart? Family and friends may have cautioned you lovingly, but your heart triumphed and you departed with bags packed. It might have involved a physical journey to another place, or it could have been a decision to alter the direction of your life, affecting your mental, emotional and spiritual well-being. Perhaps home life became impossible and you felt obliged to move out, or a relationship crumbled and you left for new pastures; maybe your church had lost its attraction, or the Christian life in its totality seemed to be a pointless exercise in a busy world.

You might be looking back now, having returned from your adventure. Your situation may look much the same as it did when you left, yet you know it's totally different because you are changed by your experiences. Body, mind and spirit will have been affected in their own ways.

Imagine that Jesus travelled with you from the day you started. God watches over us when the plan's going well and when we wander off the path, or when we find ourselves in trouble. Can you see any God-moments in the whole adventure when you were preserved from serious harm, or given help when none looked likely? Can you remember where you were when you came to your senses and understood that you and God belong together?

It is unlikely you would have regained your sight and perspective without God's involvement. In the story Jesus told, no reason was given as to why the son demanded his share and decided to leave home. We may not know exactly what caused us to strike out on our own, or remember whether we fully considered the rightness of our plan before going, but in the parable, the father was not concerned with the reasons for the child leaving. Forgiveness wipes the slate clean.

Father God welcomes us back as soon as we turn around. The parable about the lost child relates to all believers in some way, because we all wander off. There are times when our attitudes prompt us to make potentially harmful decisions, but God will help us to recover our senses, to head for home and be welcomed by the One who loves us completely.

Once you were back in the fold in a physical sense, do you remember the reception you were given? Friends and family may have welcomed you back gladly, or the reactions may have been a little muted, with some reluctance or enmity, as displayed by the elder son in the parable – see verses 25 to 30. If you were a lapsed believer for a while and now you have returned, have your Christian friends and associates welcomed you back?

These are issues you could discuss with Jesus; ask Him how to deal with them. As you reflect on how God has put a new path before you, with opportunity for you to use the things you learned in your time away, consider how God uses all experiences to shape our future. You may end up sharing the lessons you learned on your travels with other children of God as we live our lives in the world.

In your conversation with Jesus, maybe you have questions about reinstatement and the forgiveness of God; or how you and He will spend the future together, so your relationship stays healthy. You could ask how He was helping you while you were away; or how it is that no one is ever too far away, or in too deep, to be rescued and brought home. It is those who are lost He wants to find and save.[65]

The conversation

Imagine meeting Jesus to talk about His unconditional love. You could meet in the place where you came to your senses, or in the place where you feel happiest now you're back. It will be a fun-filled meeting with Him, for His reunions are joyful experiences. Why not let the Spirit start the conversation by showing you what it means for you, and for all followers of God, to be the beneficiaries of God's love, and how that love shows itself in our lives daily? Then, resting in the Spirit's peace, you can respond to Jesus as you feel led.

A prayer to finish

Father God, thank You that when I wandered from Your way, You never left me; and then,

---

[65] See Luke 19:10.

after the Spirit intervened, You watched over my journey home in safety.

I am glad there is joy in heaven when I return to You and I thank You for my reinstatement, and for Your celebrating my return. By Your Spirit, guide my feet in the right way as I commit my future to You. Amen.

9
If You're Willing

A man with leprosy came and knelt before him and said,
'Lord, if you are willing, you can make me clean.'
Jesus reached out his hand and touched the man. 'I am
willing,' he said. 'Be clean!' Immediately he was cleansed of
his leprosy. Then Jesus said to him, 'See that you don't tell
anyone. But go, show yourself to the priest and offer the
gift Moses commanded, as a testimony to them.'[66]

This question has been asked down the ages. Is God
always willing to heal? The man with leprosy knew who
he was talking to, since he called Him 'Lord' and he knew
Jesus had the power to heal, for he said, 'You can make me
clean.' But what he really needed to know was, would
Jesus be willing to heal him?

We know from Scripture that Jesus did heal in all
circumstances, but the leper didn't know that. Perhaps he
was so ashamed of his illness that he had to check with
Jesus to see if he was worthy to receive the blessing of
being healed; would Jesus stoop that low?

People ask the same question today: 'Lord, are You
willing to heal me?' This may be the result of how we view
ourselves, wondering if we're important enough to be

---

[66] Matthew 8:2-4.

healed. Is our thought, 'Other people are healed, but not me'? Do we secretly think 'I don't deserve healing'?

The Gospels are full of healing stories. It is true no one has the right to be healed, but God's love and mercy knows no boundaries. Jesus answered the leper's question with an unqualified 'Yes', and commanded his healing – and immediately the man was 'cleansed of his leprosy'. Then Jesus told him to visit the priest and obey the requirements of the law, so that the man could be reintegrated fully into society and join collective worship in the synagogue. Jesus wanted the man to receive all that God had planned for him, not just the physical healing, but also healing for his emotional, mental and spiritual health.

Since Jesus is 'the same yesterday and today and for ever',[67] it should not surprise us when we see miraculous healings today among God's people; the difficult questions and the doubts tend to arise when we see others who are not healed, or would appear not to be healed, for no obvious reason.

Why some people are healed and others are not remains one of humanity's most challenging questions. Christians believe God will always answer a plea for mercy and healing – that is His character – but His response will come in the way that benefits us the most, which may not be what we ask for or expect. Sometimes our perception of our need, which is what we may pray for, does not correspond with God's view of our need, and this can lead to disappointment – but God sees the whole picture and knows us completely, so He will heal us in the

[67] Hebrews 13:8.

way that is best for us; our challenge is to trust that He knows best.

Sometimes the healing is immediate, as in this story, but in other circumstances it can take longer, for there may be blocks to healing which have to be dealt with before the complete healing can be received. Such blocks might be, for example, a lack of forgiveness for an offence committed against us, or a sin committed that we have not admitted. There are many kinds of blocks and they need to be spiritually discerned. Removing blocks in the healing process are healings in themselves, and they need to be seen as such, otherwise we might think our prayer is not answered when, in reality, it is being worked out. Healing received in stages does require our trust, humility and patience, but with the Spirit's help, we can do this.

The most painful and distressing times are when we or our loved ones do not appear to receive healing after prayers have been said. In such cases, this can cause us to question our faith, or even question the goodness of God. But one of God's names is Jehovah Rapha, which means 'I am the LORD, who heals you'[68] and there is no condition or prevarication about this, so perhaps we can ask the Spirit to help us to believe this, even if we don't understand it, for Jesus demonstrated His desire to heal by healing the sick in great numbers during His time on earth.

Healing is such a big part of God's character and of who He is that He is always willing and able to heal – it can be no other way, and while there will be an explanation for absence of healing, sometimes we may have to wait for

---

[68] Exodus 15:26.

God to reveal it. Sometimes people may tell us we do not have enough faith to be healed, but it's never just about faith, for God is the giver of faith and He will respond if we pray for more faith. It is the Holy Spirit who will help us to discern the will of God in the healing process.

Thoughts for reflection before we talk with God

Imagine what it would be like to be in the crowd when the leper comes to Jesus and begs Him on his knees. You can see how ill he is, you can hear his desperation; he knows that this could be his last chance of getting better. He has lost everything already – he is ceremonially unclean and barred from the synagogue, he's a social outcast and lives outside the town.

You can see Jesus as He addresses the man. What is the first thing that makes an impression on you? That Jesus has healed the man right in front of your eyes, or that He reached out and touched the man? Does the fact He touched the man shock you? Has Jesus shocked you by doing something unexpected? Does His unpredictability change your perception of Him?

This healing is one where Jesus healed the leper with very little said; there was no talk of faith, no questions, just a command for healing and instructions to visit the priest. This is similar to when Jesus healed the man with the shrivelled hand;[69] there was no conversation. In other healings, there is more interaction. Jesus commended several people for their faith, such as Bartimaeus[70] or the

---

[69] See Luke 6:6-10.
[70] See Mark 10:46-52

woman with an issue of blood,[71] saying their faith had healed them. When friends brought the paralysed man on a mat to Jesus, He commended the friends' faith.[72] In the healing of the demon-possessed boy, Jesus told His disciples only prayer could bring about some healings,[73] and other times Jesus was heard to ask questions before He healed, such as, 'Do you want to get well?'[74] Perhaps Jesus is unpredictable because He looks at our hearts;[75] yet when He looks at us, with mercy, compassion and understanding, He ensures we receive healing in the way that best meets our needs.

There is so much we don't understand, so many questions about healing we could ask. Perhaps you or a loved one have been ill and not healed, and your hope and faith have been shaken. One factor we need to keep in focus is that God works in the eternal dimension, while we live in the physical world that is bound by time. Sometimes, when people are in extreme circumstances, Jesus can heal by replacing fear with a sense of peace, reminding His followers that His 'Father's house has many rooms' and that He will come back and take us to be with Him forever.[76] So while we may not be able to understand all the things that affect the outpouring of God's healing grace, with the help of the Spirit, we can keep our eyes on Jesus and trust Him even when we don't understand.

---

71 See Luke 8:43-48.

72 See Mark 2:5.

73 See Mark 9:29.

74 John 5:6.

75 See 1 Samuel 16:7.

76 John 14:1-4.

The conversation

Back with Jesus, imagine that as the healed man quickly departs, Jesus turns to you. There are large crowds milling around and Jesus is going to Capernaum next, but He wants to talk with you first. So He finds a quiet spot away from the crowd, a natural grotto nearby, and you sit down; it's heaven being beside Him. As He encourages you to speak, perhaps you could ask the Spirit to give you words that witness to the wonder of God's healing power in action today, and let you receive a new revelation about how the God of love heals us.

A prayer to finish

Father God, I thank You that You are always willing to heal, even if it is in a way that is not what I expect or have requested. You always have my best interests at heart and I trust You, Lord.

May the Holy Spirit align my heart with Yours, so that I may reach that place of wholeness and restoration, where You are. Thank You for healing me in this world, and preparing me for new life with You in the next. Amen.

10
Fearfully and Wonderfully Made

For you created my inmost being;
you knit me together in my mother's womb.
I praise you because I am fearfully and wonderfully made;
your works are wonderful,
I know that full well.
My frame was not hidden from you
when I was made in the secret place,
when I was woven together in the depths of the earth.
Your eyes saw my unformed body;
all the days ordained for me were written in your book
before one of them came to be.
How precious to me are your thoughts, God!
How vast is the sum of them!
Were I to count them,
they would outnumber the grains of sand –
when I awake, I am still with you.[77]

This is a very personal psalm by David. He is aware that
God Himself has made him and ordained the span of his
life before he was born. God has created his inmost being,
which is the centre of our emotions and moral sensitivity,
and this is the part of a person that God scrutinises when
He examines what we have become. David pictures

---

[77] Psalm 139:13-18.

himself being knitted together by God as he is made in his mother's womb, a combination of the component parts of body, mind and spirit.

Even with all the science and technology now in the world, we do not know how the whole person is made. God's works are so wonderful, and complicated, that they are beyond our human capacity to understand, so David responds in the only way he can – he praises God with awe and wonder and says, 'I am fearfully and wonderfully made.'

After considering how his life began, David reflects on the span of his life, noting that all his days were ordained and recorded in God's book before life even started. In his humility, David is able to recognise the sovereignty of God when it comes to life and death, and his reference to when he awakes even foretells God's presence beyond death.

It is humanity's loss when we live in the belief that there is no higher Presence to whom we owe an allegiance. When God is not acknowledged as the One who gives and sustains life, the history of the world advances without a full measure of the wisdom, grace and mercy that is necessary for a just and righteous existence.

David also spoke for Jesus when he said, 'I am fearfully and wonderfully made.' We are made in the image of God, and Jesus was fully human, so He was made as we are made. The wonder of our creation in human form is truly demonstrated in Jesus, because through the life Jesus lived on earth, He brought to completion God's plan for the salvation of the world.

In verses 23 and 24 of this psalm, David says, 'Search me, God, and know my heart; test me and know my anxious thoughts. See if there is any offensive way in me, and lead me in the way everlasting.' Do we think about saying David's prayer so that we can come closer to God as we consider the humanity of Jesus?

Imagine being an observer at the birth of Jesus. It would be very different from the images shown on Christmas cards, since it would be very dark in the stable, dimly lit by a lantern near to Mary, dirty and dusty, without any birthing facilities and probably minimum help. Possibly there were animals sharing the accommodation while Mary was using a manger as the crib.

Shortly after the birth, some shepherds visit, explaining that they have been visited in the fields by an angel who told them about the birth of a saviour, and the angel was joined by a delegation from the heavenly host who were all praising God. Now they are here, excited and full of praise.

Perhaps we might take some time to think about the baby Jesus, fully human and born to Mary; one of His names is '"Immanuel" (which means "God with us")'.[78]

Imagine you see Him in one of the towns – what would His early life be like? What might it be like living with Mary and Joseph and His brothers and sisters in Nazareth? He lives there for thirty years and works for many years in the carpenter's shop. Imagine how He would fit in as a boy and as a man, without sinning; when,

---

[78] Matthew 1:23.

as a boy of twelve, He gets left behind in Jerusalem; how He might relate to His brothers and sisters who are younger than Him; how Mary might relate to Him knowing He is the Messiah; is she restless while waiting for Him to start His ministry?

Then, after His baptism, He spends time in the wilderness; what might it be like having such deep union with the Father all the time? Now He is an adult and busy teaching, preaching and healing the crowds.

Do you wonder why Jesus has a greater affinity with Peter, James and John during His ministry? Is it their humour, their insight, their heart for the kingdom?

The Bible stories show Jesus as someone who liked being in company with others, enjoying time with family, friends and disciples. He loved talking to people He met while travelling and His conversations were always full of wisdom and good sense, even when challenging those who opposed Him. He had heavenly work to do, but the Gospels tell us a lot about His human relationships, as well as His relationship with His Father. How can we relate to Jesus the man, Him without sin, us being sinners? We can humble ourselves before Him, but also consider Him our brother. His humanity and sacrifice opened the way for us to enter into the presence of God, and He showed us how to live, to laugh, to love our neighbours and forgive those who hurt us. 'The fullness' of God lives within Him,[79] so we know what God is like. At the same time, Jesus the man has shown what is possible for humanity, and we can be encouraged by knowing we are truly 'fearfully and wonderfully made'.

---

[79] Colossians 2:9.

Ask the Holy Spirit to guide you in your conversation with Jesus. The questions suggested above cover some practical aspects of His life, but maybe the Spirit will suggest you ask about a particular characteristic of Jesus that will be extra special to you. Many of us wonder what He, His disciples and friends did when no one was watching and they were just having fun on their own. Perhaps He will tell us if we ask?

The conversation

Imagine meeting Jesus in His home in Nazareth for a conversation. It could be before His baptism and the start of His ministry, or after. You could sit in the carpentry shop where Joseph and Jesus worked, on chairs Jesus has made. There would be tools lying on surfaces and part-made implements, household items and furniture around the shop. And as you settle down, receiving the gentle guiding of the Spirit, perhaps you could ask Jesus about that time when 'he made himself nothing by taking the very nature of a servant, being made in human likeness',[80] and came to live among us. And as you listen to His reply, let the Spirit teach you about one of the habits Jesus adopted while He lived on earth, which pleased Father God in heaven.

A prayer to finish

Dear Father, when I think of Jesus and His time on earth, knowing He lived without sin, I

---

[80] Philippians 2:7.

praise You with awe and wonder. It is impossible for me to live as He did, but with grace, I can grow to become more like Him, little by little.

And as I consider how I am made, with body, mind and spirit, just as He was, I pray I will be open to the Holy Spirit as my teacher and guide, so that my life will give clear evidence of just who I am following. Amen.

11
Father, Forgive Them

*Two other men, both criminals, were also led out with him
to be executed. When they came to the place called the
Skull, they crucified him there, along with the criminals –
one on his right, the other on his left. Jesus said, 'Father,
forgive them, for they do not know what they are doing.'
And they divided up his clothes by casting lots.*[81]

While Jesus was hanging on the cross, it was indescribably
painful to talk, or even take a breath, yet He spoke on
seven occasions. In doing this, He showed how important
He considered His words to be, and believers have prayed
over them down the years. Most of the words are quite
personal to Him, but on two of the seven occasions, His
words could be seen as a final gift of love to His disciples
and the believers of the future. One is the affirmation that
it is never too late to be saved, as the repentant criminal
discovered,[82] and the other is when Jesus forgave the
people responsible for His crucifixion, which highlights
the importance Jesus attaches to forgiving those who sin
against us.

---

[81] Luke 23:32-34.
[82] See Luke 23:42-43.

During His ministry, Peter asked Jesus how often he should forgive his brother when he sinned against him, and Jesus said, 'Not seven times, but seventy-seven times.'[83] Jesus also spoke about forgiveness during the Sermon on the Mount when, after teaching His disciples how to pray, Jesus said that if we 'forgive other people when they sin against' us, our 'heavenly Father will also forgive' us, but if we 'do not forgive others their sins', our 'Father will not forgive' us our sins.[84]

Jesus identified a willingness to forgive others as one of the most important characteristics we need for entry into eternal life. His forgiving words on the cross aligned with what He preached, for Jesus was without sin throughout His life and had no need to be forgiven, but while on the cross, He asked His Father to forgive the people who killed Him unjustly, thereby showing us that forgiveness is possible in any circumstance.

In forgiving His accusers, Jesus showed many of the characteristics that define forgiveness. It is given without conditions, it is one-sided and it asks for nothing in exchange. It needs no acknowledgement to be effective and it is the person who forgives who is set free. Although humankind cannot truly forgive without the involvement of the Holy Spirit, that involvement is never withheld. There is no limit on the number of people we can forgive, or the number of offences forgiven, and it's never too late. But it's not a natural attitude and rarely the first response when we are sinned against. Forgiveness does not dilute the seriousness of the offence, or let the offender get away

---

[83] Matthew 18:22.
[84] Matthew 6:14-15.

with it. It doesn't alter the fact that the offender will face judgement in the future, if not on earth then at the day of judgement if they don't repent. But it does break the cord that binds the offender to the victim. Forgiveness brings freedom.

As we grow to be more like Jesus, we learn to take small steps on the road of forgiveness. It is seldom an instant fix or a quick decision. More often, it is a long road on which we tread gingerly; sometimes we don't reach the end, but any distance along the road brings a blessing to us.

And we always walk with Jesus when we travel on the forgiveness road, which makes it a safe way.

Thoughts for reflection before we talk with God

Imagine you are a bystander at the cross when Jesus was crucified with two others. There is a group of women standing there with a man, and the soldiers are overseeing the execution; you wish you were elsewhere, but you feel compelled to stay. You listen to the crucified men as they struggle to speak a few words; it is so difficult for them that their words must be very important. On one occasion, all three men speak in turn. You also hear Jesus ask why He is forsaken, and you hear Him ask His Father to forgive His accusers, because they don't know what they're doing; you hear Him settle His mother's future. Then Jesus calls out He is thirsty and the soldiers offer Him a sponge, and, then, 'It is finished.' Jesus commits His spirit to His Father and dies.[85]

---

[85] See Luke 23:39-43; Matthew 27:46; Luke 23:34; John 19:26-30; Luke 23:46.

Are you shocked and angry by what you have seen, or afraid? Perhaps curious too – how could Jesus forgive such an injustice?

God raised Jesus to life on the third day and then Jesus went about meeting His disciples. They were amazed and excited to see Jesus again, and perhaps were wondering what their future might look like, but one would suppose none of them were thinking much about forgiving the people who had crucified their Lord. We are not told if the subject was discussed while Jesus lived upon the earth, prior to His ascension into heaven, but we can talk with Jesus about this and see what we can learn from His example.

If we forgive others, we are set free, and we will receive the forgiveness we need when we get things wrong. Yet forgiving others is difficult, possibly because we usually give gifts to people we like or love, whereas forgiveness is given to people who have hurt us or we feel alienated from. Sometimes we hold on to our hurts and find reasons to avoid forgiving someone else. Why not look back over your life and ask yourself about the times when you did forgive a wrong that was done against you, and the positive effect it had on your life? Conversely, perhaps there are offences that have not yet been forgiven? There can be many reasons for this – perhaps thinking it's too small to matter, or being reluctant to ask the Spirit to help us; perhaps it's too embarrassing to go back there, or it is just too painful to think about – and we bury it deep inside us, hoping the hurt will dissolve away on its own.

In some cases, we blame God for letting us get into the situation that causes us such pain, or we blame ourselves and let the offender escape responsibility. If we call on the

Holy Spirit for help, we will be equipped with power to begin the process of forgiving another for hurtful words or actions. If we blame God, which we sometimes do even though God can never be to blame, Jesus will show us how to deal with this. If we say, 'I can never forgive myself,' Jesus can help us with that too. A conversation with Jesus about forgiveness can be a life-changing experience.

The conversation

Imagine you're meeting with the risen Jesus beside the lake in Galilee to have a conversation about forgiveness. The trauma of the cross has passed, forgiveness has been given to those responsible, and you see Jesus is totally at peace. So, leaning on the Spirit, why not talk with Jesus about His example of forgiveness from the cross, and what He would wish His followers to learn and practise in their daily walk.

A prayer to finish

Lord Jesus, Your words of forgiveness from the cross show us it is possible to forgive even the worst of offences. Forgive me, please, when I have not loved You, and have not forgiven my neighbour. Fill me afresh with Your Spirit, I pray, so I may live in the love that leads to forgiveness. Amen.

12
Mary

Now Mary stood outside the tomb crying. As she wept, she
bent over to look into the tomb and saw two angels in
white, seated where Jesus' body had been, one at the head
and the other at the foot.
They asked her, 'Woman, why are you crying?'
'They have taken my Lord away,' she said, 'and I don't
know where they have put him.' At this, she turned round
and saw Jesus standing there, but she did not realise that it
was Jesus.
He asked her, 'Woman, why are you crying? Who is it you
are looking for?'
Thinking he was the gardener, she said, 'Sir, if you have
carried him away, tell me where you have put him, and I
will get him.'
Jesus said to her, 'Mary.'
She turned towards him and cried out in Aramaic,
'Rabboni!' (which means 'Teacher').
Jesus said, 'Do not hold on to me, for I have not yet
ascended to the Father. Go instead to my brothers and tell
them, "I am ascending to my Father and your Father, to
my God and your God."'
Mary Magdalene went to the disciples with the news: 'I
have seen the Lord!' And she told them that he had said
these things to her.[86]

---

[86] John 20:11-18.

John's Gospel contains the only detailed record of the meeting at the tomb between Jesus and Mary. It will have transformed Mary's life, for how could the memory of that meeting ever fade? Mary was the first person that the resurrected Jesus appeared to. She had seemed to be insignificant in the bigger scheme of things, yet Jesus chose to meet her before anyone else. Jesus knew how much she loved Him. After He had healed her,[87] she had followed Him as a member of the group of women who supported Jesus and the Twelve, but her history and culture would have deterred her from thinking that she could be chosen for a role that might be important. Yet it was she whom Jesus met first.

This story can tell us something about God's character. At the moment just before this meeting, Mary was unknown and unnewsworthy, even though she had been healed by Jesus, for many hundreds and perhaps thousands of other people had also been healed by Him. Believers today might never have heard of Mary if it had not been for that meeting at the tomb, for all other references in the Gospels may have been included to add information about the person who was the first to meet Him.

So why did Jesus choose to meet Mary before all others? He could have chosen to meet one of the Twelve; Peter, James and John had accompanied Him when Jairus' daughter was healed, and had been invited to join Him on top of the mountain as witnesses of His transfiguration;[88] they even walked with Jesus further into

---

[87] See Luke 8:2.
[88] See Matthew 17:1-2; Mark 5:37-42.

Gethsemane after the other disciples were told to sit down and pray.[89] Possibly they could have been suitable to meet first. Perhaps Gamaliel,[90] a Pharisee and a member of the Sanhedrin[91] could have made the announcement; he was highly thought of, spoke well and would have made a good impression with those in authority. Or why did Jesus not appear to His mother, to relieve her from the pain and suffering she had been enduring in the past week?

We do not know why He chose Mary Magdalene, but His choice reminds us of an aspect of His character. God doesn't do things our way. He says His 'thoughts are not [our] thoughts, neither are [our] ways [His] ways'.[92] Jesus says 'the last will be first, and the first will be last'.[93] Paul points out God uses 'foolish things ... to shame the wise' and 'weak things ... to shame the strong' and the 'lowly things of this world ... to nullify the things' that would lay claim to being better, 'so that no one may boast before him'.[94]

Jesus has a special purpose for everyone, even for those who don't stand out in the crowd; sometimes it's very obvious, sometimes not, but God has a plan for each of us and it will be achieved. Often human opinions of worth or significance are given a greater credibility by the world than they merit, and we can be made to feel undervalued or insignificant, but God is not swayed by human opinion. The reality is that God's love for us is the true measure of

---

[89] Mark 14:32-33

[90] See Acts 5:34.

[91] The assembly of the elders of Israel.

[92] Isaiah 55:8.

[93] Matthew 20:16.

[94] 1 Corinthians 1:27-29.

our worth and significance; He knows each of us individually, and He will use us in all sorts of ways in His kingdom. Mary is a great example of this, and we can be sure God has plans for us too.

Thoughts for reflection before we talk with God

Visualise the scene on the first day of the week near the tomb. Mary is in a state of shock, confused and distressed. She has witnessed Jesus dying on the cross, gone with Joseph to the tomb, watched him bury Jesus and roll the big stone across the entrance, and now she has discovered the body has been taken from the tomb. She told the news to Peter and John and they ran to the tomb and found it as she said, but then they returned to 'where they were staying'.[95] So now she is alone again and weeping in despair. Through her tears, she sees two figures in the tomb, seated where the body had been. They ask her a question and she repeats her story. Then she turns around and sees someone else in the garden, who starts with the same question: 'Why are you crying?' Mary thinks He is the gardener and tells the story again; then Jesus says to her, 'Mary.'[96]

Has there been a time in your life when you have felt, or been made to feel, invisible or insignificant; when your presence was overshadowed by more dominant members of a group, when people didn't accept what you said, then you looked for answers, but you asked the wrong questions? Mary seemed to be caught in such a situation, until Jesus met her and asked her to deliver important

---

[95] John 20:10.
[96] John 20:15-16.

news. After Mary initially greeted Jesus as '"Rabboni!" (which means "Teacher")',[97] might they have talked as old friends, until she left to take the message to His followers?

You can talk intimately with Jesus too. All of us can. We could tell Him about the times when we felt invisible, so He can heal those memories; we can talk about some of the good times, when being recognised for our value made a difference in our life.

Perhaps at times when we have felt invisible or unimportant, Jesus has been working through us by His Spirit without our being aware, and using us as His messenger, or involving us as His helper in someone else's healing. Why not look back to events that have occurred in your life that you didn't quite understand and see what you can notice? Talking with Jesus can reveal the truth.

The conversation

Imagine you're in the garden with Jesus. Mary has left and it is just you and Jesus together. He calls you by the name that is special to you and you can see in His eyes His joy at being with you. Perhaps, like Mary, to express your love you would have liked to hug Him. With the help of the Spirit, why not ask Jesus to show you how He has been helping you in your life, day by day, and how you are truly significant in the building of His kingdom.

---

[97] John 20:16.

A prayer to finish

Dear Lord, You are so faithful. Thank You for loving me all the time. When I feel insignificant or unappreciated, even when I feel invisible, You affirm me by calling my name and letting me dwell in Your presence. Your willingness to hold me close shows me I am truly significant in Your sight.

I thank You, Lord, for the story of Mary Magdalene, for You loved Mary, not for what she had done, but for who she was, and the same applies to me. Holy Spirit, please teach me to keep my eyes fixed on Jesus – that I will be sensitive to His call and useful in His service. Amen.

13
Jesus Is the Only Way

*Thomas said to him, 'Lord, we don't know where you are
going, so how can we know the way?'
Jesus answered, 'I am the way and the truth and the life.
No one comes to the Father except through me. If you really
know me, you will know my Father as well. From now on,
you do know him and have seen him.'* [98]

*If you love me, keep my commands. And I will ask the
Father, and he will give you another advocate to help you
and be with you for ever – the Spirit of truth. The world
cannot accept him, because it neither sees him nor knows
him. But you know him, for he lives with you and will be in
you.* [99]

When Moses met God in the burning bush on Mount
Horeb and received instructions on how to rescue the
people of Israel from Egypt, one of the first questions he
asked God concerned His name. What should he say if
they asked who had sent him? God replied to Moses that
His name is 'I AM WHO I AM' and that he should tell the
people, 'I AM has sent me to you.' [100] So when Jesus made

---

[98] John 14:5-7.
[99] John 14:15-17.
[100] Exodus 3:14.

seven declarations during His ministry which started with the words 'I am',[101] God was again talking directly to His people about Himself. All seven declarations have words immediately following them that expand on what Jesus has said, but while six recite the benefits that flow from the description He gives of Himself, one declaration differs slightly from the rest, in that there is a word of warning attached. When Jesus said He is 'the way and the truth and the life', He added, 'No one comes to the Father except through me.'

When sin entered into the relationship between God and humankind, we were banished from God's presence. Our only way back was to find a sufficient sacrifice to atone for the sins of the whole world, which was impossible for us, so God took pity and provided one. God gave us Jesus, and said that 'whoever believes in him shall not perish but have eternal life'.[102] Because Jesus was fully human as well as fully God, and lived on earth without sin, He was the perfect sacrifice, and by His death our relationship with God is restored. But it is only through faith in Jesus that we are made righteous before God, and thus our salvation is in Him alone. We are worthy because we are covered by His righteousness.

So access to the Father has to be through Jesus. Some people trust and believe in God, but do not fully understand the relationship between Father and Son, so they worship Father God but are offended by Jesus the Son and look away from Him. There can be many reasons for this, but it is not the way to gain salvation. Where this is

---

[101] See John 6:35; 8:12 and 9:5; 10:7; 10:11,14; 11:25; 14:6; 15:1.
[102] John 3:16.

the case and we ask for help, God will send us the Spirit of truth for our aid, and He will live within us and teach us what is true. Only the Holy Spirit can do this.

Thoughts for reflection before we talk with God

Imagine hearing Jesus talk about Himself as 'the way and the truth and the life'. When He said this to the disciples, Jesus had already shared the meal in the upper room and washed their feet, and now He was telling them He would be going away to a place they knew, that they couldn't go with Him, but He would come back later from where He'd gone. It was Thomas saying he didn't know the place, or the way, which started this part of the conversation. Jesus went on to say that if they really knew Him, they would 'know [the] Father as well'. Not stopping there, Jesus said that they did know the Father already, and had 'seen him'.[103]

When Philip asked another question, in verse 8 of John 14, confirming his lack of understanding, Jesus explained the relationship between Himself and the Father and promised the gift of the Holy Spirit.

When we talk with Jesus, we can ask Him to explain the mystery of Jesus being in the Father and the Father being in Him. We could ask Him what He means when He says that those who believe in Him 'will do the works I have been doing, and they will do even greater things than these'.[104] Jesus adds a further promise at the supper, that He will do whatever we ask in His name, so that the Father

---

[103] John 14:5-7.
[104] John 14:12.

is given the glory.[105] What is required of us if we do pray in His name?

Consider the story of the Pharisee who came to Jesus by night, Nicodemus. Here is a man who was learned, with a strong desire to know the truth, who recognised that the miraculous signs performed by Jesus showed God's involvement – yet Nicodemus couldn't make sense of what Jesus was doing. So Jesus said to him that 'no one can see the kingdom of God unless they are born again'. After Nicodemus had replied, Jesus said that 'no one can enter the kingdom of God unless they are born of water and the Spirit'.[106] Jesus was explaining to Nicodemus that there is need for a spiritual birth as well as a natural birth. Jesus was saying we are living in both the natural world and the spiritual world even now, and we need to be welcomed into the spiritual world if we are to understand Jesus when He speaks of heavenly things. Being of a religious persuasion in the natural world alone is not enough.

As you prepare to talk with Jesus, perhaps you could ask about being born again, what it involves, when it happens. You could ask Him about being born of the Spirit. Perhaps ask Him to talk about His being 'the way and the truth and the life'. And as Jesus speaks to us, the Holy Spirit teaches us and later reminds us of everything Jesus has said.[107]

---

[105] See John 14:13.

[106] John 3:3-5.

[107] See John 14:26.

The conversation

Imagine you are a helper at the Last Supper when Jesus is talking to the disciples. You've seen their feet washed and their questions have been answered, and then Jesus sees you wanting to ask something, so He takes you aside to a quiet corner and invites you to speak. Why not let the Spirit of truth bless you with the words to ask Jesus about the way to salvation, and then relax in His peace as Jesus explains what is required from those who believe in God.

A prayer to finish

Lord Jesus, when You asked the Twelve if they wanted to leave You in the way so many others had done, it was Peter who answered and asked where would they go, for the words of eternal life are with You alone[108] and Your deeds and miracles proved it daily. Lord, I would say that for myself too, for where would I go?

Thank You for giving Yourself to save me, and thank You that, because I know You, I also know the Father in heaven.

Help me to understand better what You mean when You say You are 'the way and the truth and the life', and what it means to be 'born of the Spirit'.[109] You are my teacher, Holy Spirit, and I wait for You to shine Your light

---

[108] See John 6:68.
[109] John 3:8.

*on these mysteries as You work in my life, more
and more. Amen.*

14
The Supremacy of Christ

The Son is the image of the invisible God, the firstborn over all creation. For in him all things were created: things in heaven and on earth, visible and invisible, whether thrones or powers or rulers or authorities; all things have been created through him and for him. He is before all things, and in him all things hold together. And he is the head of the body, the church; he is the beginning and the firstborn from among the dead, so that in everything he might have the supremacy. For God was pleased to have all his fullness dwell in him, and through him to reconcile to himself all things, whether things on earth or things in heaven, by making peace through his blood, shed on the cross.[110]

Paul's letter to the Colossians was written to show that Christ is all we need to gain our salvation, and that we should be on our guard against any alternative spirituality in the world that affects our understanding. The world has always had many different gods and faiths to choose from, and this remains true today. When the people of Israel were living in Egypt, there were plenty of Egyptian gods to be worshipped. In New Testament times, many Greek and Roman gods and goddesses, with their associated

---

[110] Colossians 1:15-20

temples, vied for the attention of new followers, and there were other people who worshipped angels and the heavenly bodies. These gods were content to live alongside each other, and when Christianity started, to many it seemed like just one more religion to choose from. Gods were plentiful in those days.

Yet, for the God of Israel, His position and His status were made very clear from the start: His people were to have no other gods than Him,[111] and this condition was agreed by the people when the book of the law was read at Mount Sinai.[112] So, after the resurrection of Jesus and the provision of the new covenant, whereby salvation now is through faith in Jesus alone, Paul is teaching the new believers the same message: there is one God only, who is Father, Son and Holy Spirit, and there is no other God. Believers have to be on guard against any idea, however innocent it looks, that interferes with the purity of this truth.

The passage above declares 'the supremacy' of Christ the Son. He is supreme in creation and supreme in redemption. Because God is Spirit and therefore invisible to us, God made Himself visible to human eyes in the person of Jesus Christ. Because God is three persons, with all three being absolutely equal, yet one God, Paul explains Christ has 'the supremacy' to ensure there is no misunderstanding about who has the final word on kingdom matters. Elsewhere in the Bible, Christ is described as 'the radiance of God's glory and the exact

---

[111] See Exodus 20:2-3.
[112] See Exodus 24:7.

representation of his being',[113] and Jesus Himself said, 'Anyone who has seen me has seen the Father.'[114] There is no room left for manoeuvre or discussion.

Having stated the truth clearly, Paul then expands on the pre-eminence of Jesus in every possible scenario: He is foremost in creation, in heaven and earth, in things we can see and in those we can't. There are no exceptions, anywhere, with all things 'created through him and for him'. Jesus is not limited by time, because He is before time, and He sustains all things.

He is also pre-eminent in the Church, which is the body of Christ and comprises all believers of every age. The fullness of who God is, with all His powers and attributes, lives in Jesus so that, through Him, by the shedding of His blood on the cross, He could reconcile everything to Himself, with no exception. While Adam, the first man, caused sin and death to enter the world, breaking the relationship with God and causing disharmony in the created world, Jesus brought salvation, forgiveness, life and reconciliation to humankind and the created order. This is why Jesus is everything we will ever need to gain our salvation.

These mysteries are in the Scriptures for our benefit, so we need to ask the Holy Spirit to assist us in our understanding. Then we will avoid being diverted away from truth into things that are not of God.

---

[113] Hebrews 1:3.
[114] John 14:9.

Thoughts for reflection before we talk with God

Paul tells us Christ is 'before all things'. Imagine meeting Jesus, Father and the Spirit at the planning meeting in heaven for the new creation. We are made in God's image, so what do you imagine They look like? Think about what might have been discussed as the creation plan developed and the Godhead of Father, Son and Holy Spirit decided Jesus would be supreme and Father would make all things 'through him and for him'.

We could ask what was Their reaction to the Fall and the entry of sin into the world. Or ask about the plan to save the world, when Jesus would become incarnate and actually live in the world with us. Or what was the Father doing while Jesus lived on earth until His baptism and the start of His ministry? And what about the relationship between Father and Son during the ministry of Jesus in the world, and the depth of love between them? It is God's inspired Word that has told us these things, so we can expect God to be wanting to talk to us about them.

We are also told Jesus is the 'head of ... the church' and the first member of it. In everything He is supreme and complete. Do we recognise the characteristics of Jesus in the words and actions of people in the church we attend, and in the worldwide Church, or are there attempts to dilute the truth of who He is? The apostle Paul advises against believing in or adopting any extra rules and regulations that are said to be necessary for salvation.[115] Empty worldly thinking can be added into godly teaching in order to lead people astray.

---

[115] See Colossians 2:20-23.

What does Jesus look for in His disciples, and how can we be discerning in the faith? We can ask Him about our own journey of faith and what He is planning for us. He tells us we are 'light' in the world,[116] and to be His light we need to be as pure as we can. We need to ask Him how we can avoid being deceived by the enemy. Accepting the supremacy of Christ in our head is good, but do we know His supremacy in our hearts also? Paul tells us that since we have been 'raised with Christ', we should now align our hearts and minds with heavenly things, instead of earthly things.[117]

The conversation

Imagine you're back in the planning meeting with the Godhead. There is unity between the three Persons, but Jesus is coming to talk with you, and you are being blessed with the indwelling of the Holy Spirit. With the Spirit guiding your thoughts and words, you could ask Jesus to expand on the meaning of His being supreme in creation and supreme in redemption, and how to preserve in us the truth that Jesus is all anyone needs to be saved.[118]

A prayer to finish

Gracious God, You are so great that I cannot fully comprehend how Jesus, who has the supremacy in the whole of creation, could die on the cross for me; and that He would do this

---

[116] Matthew 5:14.

[117] Colossians 3:1-2.

[118] See Acts 4:12.

if I was the only person in the world who needed to be saved. Yet I do believe this truth, and I am so very touched by Your love for me.

Lord, I pray for a deeper intimacy with Your Spirit, that I will come to be more like Jesus, day by day. Amen.

15
Greater Love Has No One

They crucified two rebels with him, one on his right and one on his left. Those who passed by hurled insults at him, shaking their heads and saying, 'So! You who are going to destroy the temple and build it in three days, come down from the cross and save yourself!' In the same way the chief priests and the teachers of the law mocked him among themselves. 'He saved others,' they said, 'but he can't save himself! Let this Messiah, this king of Israel, come down now from the cross, that we may see and believe.' Those crucified with him also heaped insults on him.[119]

Greater love has no one than this: to lay down one's life for one's friends.[120]

Crucifixion was the most cruel, humiliating and shaming form of execution. It was carried out publicly and the accusers were present to mock and taunt Jesus, while those crucified with Him also threw insults at Him. It seemed a total defeat for the Son of Man; Jesus even cried, 'My God, my God, why have you forsaken me?'[121] How could it be any worse?

---

[119] Mark 15:27-32.
[120] John 15:13.
[121] Matthew 27:46.

It is the cruelty that tends to attract much of the attention, but it also asks searching questions about God Himself. How could God allow Jesus to suffer in such a way, or abandon Him at the time He needed Him most? How could God ignore the cry from Jesus in the garden of Gethsemane?[122]

To give up one's life for another is the greatest love of all. Jesus had free will to choose what He would do, and when the decision time came, He chose to give up His life for all the people of the world – past, present and future. Jesus had lived His life without sin, so He knew He could be the atoning sacrifice for a righteous God – and if He offered His life, the price would be paid and it would be sufficient to cancel out the sins of the whole world; the demand for justice would be met and reconciliation with God could follow. But it was His choice whether or not He gave up His life for all, and 'all' included both friend and foe.

So the real heart in the story of the crucifixion is not its horror, but the love of God that put in place a plan to save humankind. Jesus suffered indescribable pain on the cross, but consider too the pain of Father, who also suffered indescribable pain in heaven while He resisted using His power to intervene before Jesus had completed His work on earth. If we focus on just one thing, we would do well to focus on the love of God. If you ever wonder if God loves you, the magnitude of the love displayed by the Father and the Son during the crucifixion should persuade you beyond doubt.

---

[122] Matthew 26:39,42.

Some people reject the faith because they are offended by the cruelty of Good Friday, or the perceived lack of compassion by God towards Jesus. This is sad, because these aspects of the crucifixion are diversions to prevent people seeing what really happened. The truth is the future of the world was totally reset by the crucifixion, because when God raised Jesus from the tomb on the third day, death and the fear of 'there's nothing else' were defeated once and for all, and all people were given the opportunity to live eternally with God.

If those seeking truth would turn their eyes to the great love God displayed on that fateful Friday, their lives would be transformed. For it would be possible to see the truth of the cross in its proper context of being the greatest act of love ever seen; and they would know they could share in the life everlasting that Jesus promises to those who believe in Him.

Thoughts for reflection before we talk with God

The foundation of the Christian faith is that Jesus died for the sins of the whole world in order to save the world. If there was no Good Friday, there would be no Easter Sunday, and all of us would still be trying to earn our own salvation. God loved us enough to send Jesus, and Jesus loved us enough to sacrifice Himself for us. There was much mockery and disdain at the cross, but still love triumphed and saved the world.

There is a spiritual battle for hearts and minds being waged even now, and believers need wisdom not to disregard or ignore reports of such a battle. The forces for truth point to what Jesus has done and proclaim that by

His death, He has saved the world. The powers of darkness in the world, and 'the spiritual forces of evil in the heavenly realms',[123] seek to distract people from the truth by pointing out the costs of sacrifice rather than the salvation that was obtained. The battle may be long and arduous until Christ comes again, but the truth will not be overcome. Love will have the final word.

There are other examples of love at work to be seen between Good Friday and the day of resurrection, and they can be celebrated. How about Mary the mother of Christ and the other women standing at the cross? They loved Jesus enough to stand by Him through the day, bearing their own pain. John the disciple also stood beside the cross, a steadfast and loyal friend, while Jesus suffered. After Jesus died, Joseph showed his love by asking Pilate for the body and, with Nicodemus, the one who had come by night, they took His body and treated it with love, respect and honour, and laid it in the tomb. Then on Sunday, Mary showed her love for Him by going to the tomb, just wanting to be near Him, as did the other women too, bringing spices. Acts of love like these inspire others to do likewise.

We learn a little about the love between Father and Son when we hear Jesus call His Father 'Abba' in Gethsemane:[124] it's a name of deep intimacy, infused with total trust, humility and obedience, and a bit like 'Daddy' in our language.

---

[123] Ephesians 6:12.
[124] Mark 14:36.

So did the Father abandon Jesus 'at three in the afternoon'?[125] What made Jesus feel He'd been forsaken? God's Word says that He will never leave us nor forsake us.[126] Did God break His promise? Surely God's character would forbid Him to do that? We cannot know, but perhaps it was connected to when God 'laid on Him the iniquity of us all',[127] causing Jesus to be unable to sense His Father's presence?

At times, we too may be unable to sense Jesus' presence when we need Him desperately. Yet Jesus cohabits our very worst despair, because He has experienced the same, and a much greater, depth of isolation. So shall we stand firm on what we do know, trust God with what we don't know and walk in faith that God will never leave us? The Spirit will surely reveal the truth to us if we ask.

The conversation

Imagine meeting Jesus in a fragrant garden to talk about the love that was so embedded in the events at the cross. There is time for you to sit together on a garden bench and enjoy each other's company. When you're settled, why not let the Spirit lead you into a conversation with Jesus about the depth of love He has for you, and for all the people on earth, and how that love shows itself in your life, even in the times when you can't sense His presence?

---

[125] Mark 15:34.
[126] See Deuteronomy 31:6 .
[127] Isaiah 53:6.

A prayer to finish

Father God, thank You for sending Jesus to pay my ransom on the cross and for sending the Holy Spirit to explain about the love that brought me salvation. May the sights and sounds of worldly activity recede, and my appreciation of Your love and faithfulness grow deeper, as I learn to be more aware of Your constant presence beside me – thank You. Amen.

Part Three
Living the Christian Life

16. A Woman Caught in Adultery – Judging and fault-finding

17. Zacchaeus – Showing our true selves

18. Call to Me – God wants to talk with us

19. Jars of Clay – God's light in us is by God's efforts

20. The Lord's Requirements – What God wants from us

21. My Times Are in Your Hands – God is Sovereign always

22. Forget the Former Things – Moving on, making change

23. Be Holy – How to aim higher

24. Follow Me – Starting again

25. Walking in the Light – Choice of lifestyle

26. Do Not Fret – Live contentedly and give anxiety to God

27. Why We're Here – God's purposes for us and His Church

28. There is No Condemnation – God's grace has set us free

29. Chariots and Horses – Relying on the wrong things

30. The Word – The truth inside the cover

16

A Woman Caught in Adultery

At dawn he appeared again in the temple courts, where all the people gathered round him, and he sat down to teach them. The teachers of the law and the Pharisees brought in a woman caught in adultery. They made her stand before the group and said to Jesus, 'Teacher, this woman was caught in the act of adultery. In the Law Moses commanded us to stone such women. Now what do you say?' They were using this question as a trap, in order to have a basis for accusing him.

But Jesus bent down and started to write on the ground with his finger. When they kept on questioning him, he straightened up and said to them, 'Let any one of you who is without sin be the first to throw a stone at her.' Again he stooped down and wrote on the ground.

At this, those who heard began to go away one at a time, the older ones first, until only Jesus was left, with the woman still standing there. Jesus straightened up and asked her, 'Woman, where are they? Has no one condemned you?'

'No one, sir,' she said.

'Then neither do I condemn you,' Jesus declared. 'Go now and leave your life of sin.'[128]

---

[128] John 8:2-11.

The story shows how quick people can be to condemn others when they are caught openly breaking the law, but are not so ready to own up when they are challenged about their own behaviour. God always looks at the hearts of people to measure their integrity, and Jesus often challenged hypocrites when they wanted to point out the sins of others while disregarding how they acted themselves. In the Sermon on the Mount, Jesus told us not to judge others or we will be judged too, and the severity of the judgement we hand out will be reflected in how we are treated when we are judged. He also taught us about the mistake of trying to deal with 'the speck of sawdust in your brother's eye' without having attended to 'the plank in your own eye'.[129]

When the accusers first asked Jesus what He thought, He just wrote in the sand, but when they persisted, Jesus disarmed the accusers with His reply, and it was their consciences that prompted them to 'go away one at a time, the older ones first'. Jesus did not condemn the accusers for their action; He asked them to examine themselves to see how they measured themselves. It appears the older people were quicker to understand the truth of what Jesus was saying, but all of them went away without a stone thrown. Jesus didn't condemn the woman either.

The story of the woman at the temple involved a crowd, but the same principle applies to us as individuals. God hasn't given anyone, even those in authority, the right to judge and condemn indiscriminately. The accusers were rigidly following the law, which demanded adulterers to be stoned to death. Jesus showed the kingdom of God had

---

[129] Matthew 7:3.

arrived, with forgiveness, grace and mercy as part of the story. If we judge others, justice requires we judge with fairness, truth and right thinking, and the Spirit will help us with these attributes, if we ask. The payback is that if we become subject to judgement at any time, the Spirit will see to it that we are judged to the same standards, and justice will be what we receive.

Thoughts for reflection before we talk with God

Imagine if you had been in the temple courts that day and seen the commotion. What if you had been one of the accusers, acting in an official capacity, and you felt an obligation to insist upon observance of the law; would you have been supporting the elder members of the group come what may, or if you had reservations, would you have spoken up? What if you had been waiting for a friend when the delegation appeared in front of Jesus and you watched the events out of curiosity to see what would happen? Imagine you hear Him challenge the accusers that the one without sin should be first to throw a stone. What would you do if you were an accuser? How would you feel if you were a bystander?

The accusers thought they had a strong case against the woman, yet by the end of the story, she was free to go. Was it because the accusers lacked integrity or had an ulterior motive? Would it have been different if there had been just one person accusing her? It might have ended differently for the accusers if they had sought guidance from Jesus when they first heard the facts from the witness; justice demands integrity and transparency in the prosecution and the defence.

Has there been a time when you were drawn into judging someone? Is your conscience uneasy, and do you wish you hadn't got involved? If we're uneasy about the outcome of a particular situation, healing and release can be obtained if we admit our part and seek God's forgiveness. He is full of justice and mercy – He doesn't condemn those who believe in Him. 'If we confess our sins, he is faithful and just and will forgive us our sins and purify us from all unrighteousness.'[130] Once sins are forgiven, they have no power to hurt, and it is never too late to pray about an injustice, or a mistake, or a regret about past involvement. We may never know the effect our prayer may have on the other people involved, but we will surely know the peace of God in our lives as we are released from the burden of carrying regrets, or the reminders from a guilty conscience.

If we ask God for wisdom so that we can live without making critical judgements about others, and for discernment so we will know if it's our place to be the one who tells another about their faults or failings, He will meet us in our asking. In the world, it's not uncommon for people to make quick judgements and accusations before knowing all the facts; sometimes we jump to conclusions too quickly, and we can get drawn into a group-led judgement. If we are prepared to ask ourselves if our conscience is clear before we judge another, we may avoid the uncomfortable challenge that God may make if we don't. We could ask Jesus to show us the way to deal with people who persuade or manoeuvre us to do things we're not totally happy about; or how to respond with

---

[130] 1 John 1:9.

compassion and generosity in situations when we take an alternative view, or wish to put forward an alternative opinion. We can ask the Holy Spirit to guide us in all things when it comes to what we talk about with Jesus.

The conversation

Imagine you're still at the temple. The accusers have gone and so has the woman; Jesus did not condone her behaviour, but neither did He condemn her, so we can trust she left restored in dignity and self-respect following her meeting with Him. In the quiet, you see Jesus sitting alone on one of the steps, so you approach Him, and He invites you to sit beside Him. Now could be a good time to have a conversation about judging and fault-finding in others, so as the Spirit leads you, why not ask Jesus if there are instances when maybe you could have withheld making a judgement, instead of pressing on, and perhaps how you could react differently if the same situation were to arise again.

A prayer to finish

Loving Jesus, You know when we fall into the trap of judging others and convince ourselves that our actions are not too bad, or that the victim will soon get over it and we needn't worry. Sometimes we blur the truth and learn to live with it.

Please will You teach me to stand on truth, with courage, if I find myself being tempted to judge another. You always use grace and truth when You make judgements; may I be like You and do the same. Amen.

17
Zacchaeus

*Jesus entered Jericho and was passing through. A man was
there by the name of Zacchaeus; he was a chief tax collector
and was wealthy. He wanted to see who Jesus was, but
because he was short he could not see over the crowd. So he
ran ahead and climbed a sycamore-fig tree to see him, since
Jesus was coming that way.*

*When Jesus reached the spot, he looked up and said to him,
'Zacchaeus, come down immediately. I must stay at your
house today.' So he came down at once and welcomed him
gladly.*

*All the people saw this and began to mutter, 'He has gone
to be the guest of a sinner.'*

*But Zacchaeus stood up and said to the Lord, 'Look, Lord!
Here and now I give half of my possessions to the poor, and
if I have cheated anybody out of anything, I will pay back
four times the amount.'*

*Jesus said to him, 'Today salvation has come to this house,
because this man, too, is a son of Abraham. For the Son of
Man came to seek and to save the lost.'*[131]

Zacchaeus wanted to see who Jesus was. Zacchaeus was
important in the city, employed by the Romans, and
wealthy, and one might have expected him to be

---

[131] Luke 19:1-10.

concentrating on increasing his wealth even more. Yet this day was different, for Zacchaeus was not working but trying to see Jesus, even to the extent of running ahead and finding a tree to climb, in order to see Him over the crowd.

Undoubtedly he would be transformed by his meeting Jesus later, but perhaps Zacchaeus was not the mercenary person he is often perceived to be when he is looking for a way to see Jesus. Imagine a new scenario: what if it was not just curiosity that prompted him to want to see Jesus? His behaviour seems to indicate it was more than a passing thought, for he took the trouble to run ahead and find a tree that he was physically able to climb, and which gave him a good view of the procession. Such action for a man of his official position risked ridicule and loss of dignity, yet this is what he decided to do.

What might have caused this? Had Zacchaeus already started a relationship with God, and this story is telling us of the finale? Zacchaeus was employed to do a job that expected him to conform to accepted ways of working, and he knew his job carried a bad reputation; perhaps he was already changing and he wanted to reveal the new Zacchaeus, but he didn't know how to announce his turnabout, so he just did his job and hid his true self.

People in the street were saying Jesus had healed a blind man as He entered the city.[132] Perhaps Zacchaeus wondered if Jesus could help him become the person he wanted to be, the person he thought God had created him to be? When Jesus reached the tree, He looked up and told Zacchaeus to 'come down immediately', as He wished to visit his house that day. If getting help from Jesus to

---

[132] See Luke 18:35-43.

change was the plan, it certainly worked. Zacchaeus was overwhelmed with joy. Jesus could see the real person inside and was not misled by the label of his being a tax collector.

As Zacchaeus welcomed Jesus into his house, the people watched and began to criticise, but what they couldn't see was the total change in Zacchaeus as he became the person God created him to be. After the meal, he gave half his possessions to the poor and promised generous restitution to anyone he had cheated.

Jesus recognised Zacchaeus as one descended from Abraham, as in being a Jew, but also a person seeking the truth. Through meeting Jesus, Zacchaeus became the complete person God wanted him to be. People like Zacchaeus were the reason Jesus came to earth – and He continues His mission today: He comes 'to seek and to save the lost'.

Thoughts for reflection before we talk with God

Imagine you are among the people in Jericho when Jesus visits on His way to Jerusalem. The city is very crowded because Jesus has a large following, but you can see Zacchaeus, the chief tax collector, near you. Everyone knows he is wealthy and people assume his wealth has been obtained through cheating, or at the least by unfair process. You watch Zacchaeus trying to get to the front of the crowd; he's so short he can't see Jesus over their heads, but no one is giving way. He's obviously not popular. You wonder why a man like Zacchaeus would be interested in someone like Jesus.

Zacchaeus has gone ahead and climbed a tree. You can see Jesus passing the tree when suddenly He stops and looks up at Zacchaeus. He tells him to 'come down immediately', as He must visit his house. So you watch them go to his house for a meal and Zacchaeus welcomes Jesus enthusiastically. It appears Jesus is not put off by what Zacchaeus might have done in the past, or by associating with someone of his reputation.

Now there's a commotion: Zacchaeus is standing and making a speech. Apparently he has said that right now, he gives half of what he owns to the needy, and if he has cheated people during his dealings with them, he will pay it back fourfold. How amazing is that – the tax collector giving up half of what he owns and promising restitution to those he has cheated. Now Jesus is saying to the tax collector that salvation has come to his house because Zacchaeus is also 'a son of Abraham'.

Are you living your life as the person God created you to be? God gives each of us talents, gifts, personality and faith, so that we can live faithful lives in community with others, but sometimes we lose sight of this. Do people see the real you on display, or is there a façade that hides who you are? You would not be alone, for many of us hide our true selves with a disguise of some kind. Sometimes, when we fear we may lose the respect of people, or we might be teased, criticised or ridiculed for our faith or beliefs, be they long established or of recent revelation, we can pretend to be someone else so as to protect ourselves from unkind words. Yet maybe a helping hand is all we need to make the change.

Jesus will help us if we feel we are not displaying our true self to others we meet. We could ask Him how this has come about, and how to make the change, or at least how to make a start. If changing our behaviour and being true to our self will cause anxiety to those closest to us, we could ask Jesus to go ahead of us and prepare the ground, so that love and understanding will permeate future relations. We could ask Him if there are any circumstances where restitution might be appropriate, and what that might consist of. Perhaps we could take time to ponder if the story resonates with us in any way, and whether any of the questions reflect what we feel.

The conversation

Now you're back in Jericho. Imagine pushing through the crowd as you try to catch up with Jesus after He leaves Zacchaeus. He's about to tell the listeners another parable, with people milling all around, but He sees you coming towards Him and quickly finds a quiet place for you to sit and talk. As you sit together, why not listen for the Spirit guiding you into a discussion with Jesus about the freedom that comes from living a faithful life in the open, and how that could inspire you to welcome Jesus into your house today.

A prayer to finish

Lord, thank You that You see the truth in me. You are not deceived by outward appearances or disguises, and You are happy to stay with me every day. Thank You that I can start to be the person You made me to be and You give me permission to remove things that conceal the true me.

Teach me, please, to be open about who I am, and to present myself 'to God as one approved, a worker who does not need to be ashamed and who correctly handles the word of truth'.[133] Amen.

---

[133] 2 Timothy 2:15.

18
Call to Me

'This is the covenant that I will make with the people of Israel
after that time,' declares the LORD.
'I will put my law in their minds
and write it on their hearts.
I will be their God,
and they will be my people.'[134]

Call to me and I will answer you and tell you great and
unsearchable things you do not know.[135]

These verses are memorable because they contain words of hope and encouragement from God to all generations for all times. They were written by Jeremiah to the Israelites before the destruction of Jerusalem and the journey into exile, and the purpose was to encourage the people that they would still have a part to play in God's plan after the exile had ended. Most of the book of Jeremiah is focused on judgement, because God's people had shown repeatedly that they were incapable of observing the covenant they made with God at Mount

---

[134] Jeremiah 31:33.
[135] Jeremiah 33:3.

Sinai, and Jeremiah is continually warning that there would be a reckoning. Indeed, all the prophets in the Bible had the same task, which was to call people to account for their disobedience and to warn them of the consequences if they failed to change their ways.

Eventually, disaster did occur in Jeremiah's time, with Jerusalem destroyed and the people sent into exile in Babylon. However, chapters 31 to 33, often referred to as the 'book of consolation', contain a message of hope and deliverance. The coming of the Messiah had been foretold since the beginning of the world and Jeremiah was chosen to announce the new covenant that God would make with His people. Jesus is the mediator of the new covenant,[136] and it is through Him that its blessings are secured.

Jeremiah 31:33 explains how and why the relationship between God and His people evolved into one that was so much more intimate than previously, because now the law is put in minds and written on hearts. God is now in a personal relationship with each of us and we can know we are His special people.

Jeremiah 33:3 is the effect of the new relationship. God now speaks to His people on an individual basis, inviting them to have an intelligent conversation with Him, where He can explain deep matters of eternal importance. God is offering to share the secrets of His heart with us. This communication is made possible through the power of the Holy Spirit. This invitation releases us from the limits of the material world and moves us into the unlimited space of the spiritual world. This is a dialogue, where God will

---

[136] See Hebrews 9:15.

listen to us and talk with us and we can be assured of His attention. It's like He will have eye contact with us.

When Jesus walked on earth, He told his disciples that they were friends, not servants, if they did what He commanded, because servants weren't told their 'master's business'. To emphasise the point, He said they were His friends because He had shared with them everything He had learned from His Father.[137] So this change in the nature of the relationship is the result of the promise written in Jeremiah, and leads to Father God's offer to talk to us about 'great and unsearchable things'. Since God wants to enter into such a conversation, we can step outside the limits we set ourselves and begin to appreciate the vastness of God and our place within His creation and plan. It is for us to accept God's offer and meet Him for a conversation. There is no reluctance on God's part – He will listen to us, whatever our situation, wherever we are.

Thoughts for reflection before we talk with God

Have you got a question about God that you cannot get out of your mind, or an irritating thought that won't go away, in spite of your efforts to forget about it and move on? Is there something that you regret deeply, but cannot see a way of recovering from its effects? Is there anxiety in your heart that is causing you to be afraid, or prevents you from acting, or weighs you down so much that you can't see a future for yourself? Talking with God is a sure way of starting the healing process.

---

[137] John 15:14-15.

Reading the story of Martha and Mary and the death of Lazarus[138] can be helpful. Imagine the sequence of events when Jesus arrived. Both sisters had questions for Jesus and He made time to talk to them individually and answer them. They were deep questions about life and death, and Jesus told Martha He is 'the resurrection and the life'.[139] When He met Mary and saw her weeping, He responded to her grief without words. He was 'deeply moved'[140] and asked where Lazarus had been buried. The people took Him to the tomb, and there He wept. Showing His own sense of loss and sadness, He shared in their grief and they comforted each other. God meets us where we are, whatever our situation, even when we cannot express our feelings verbally. He may not use words, but He will communicate in the way that meets our need.

Friends are able to speak lovingly about subjects that may be painful. The Holy Spirit will be in our conversation with Jesus as He guides our hearts and thoughts in deep places. Martha and Mary talked with Him about the death of their beloved brother, and Jesus spoke to them about resurrection, and about believing. We can trust Him that all things are eligible for discussion. Is there a question you would like to ask, but are worried what people might think if they heard you? Are there doubts in you about the death and resurrection of Jesus? Are you uncertain about the way to eternal life? Or how life began? Or what the alternative is to eternal life with God at the end of time?

---

[138] See John 11:1-44.
[139] Verse 25.
[140] Verse 33; see also verse 38.

With the guiding of the Holy Spirit, we can be bold in the big questions we ask God to discuss with us. We may have personal experiences we wish to understand better. Jesus can go back into our past and heal our hurts and wounds; He can remove our guilt and wash away our shame. He knows us intimately and God is not limited by time – He can do more than we can possibly want or imagine.[141]

The questions the Holy Spirit prompts us to ask will be those our heart seeks to know. Why not consider what you would like to talk to Jesus about, so you're ready for when you meet?

The conversation

Imagine meeting Jesus for a conversation, sitting together as you might with a best friend. As it was for Martha and Mary, it could be in a place tainted with sadness, but you may prefer a place of learning, like a school classroom, where you can sit at adjacent desks. It's quiet and private, perfect for talking, so whether you want to ask something very profound or something very simple, the Spirit will help you to express your thoughts in words, and Jesus will look at you lovingly as He tells you what He wants to share with you today.

A prayer to finish

Dear God, thank You for inviting me to talk with You and promising to answer me.

---

[141] See Ephesians 3:20.

Sometimes I need courage to call out, but I know Your Spirit will make our conversation possible.

I am changed by our conversations. You help me to understand bigger and deeper things about Your plan and purpose for me on earth, and in the new creation of the future.

Thank You for trusting me with 'great and unsearchable things'. I pray I will use them wisely. Amen.

19
Jars of Clay

We do not use deception, nor do we distort the word of God. On the contrary, by setting forth the truth plainly we commend ourselves to everyone's conscience in the sight of God. And even if our gospel is veiled, it is veiled to those who are perishing. The god of this age has blinded the minds of unbelievers, so that they cannot see the light of the gospel that displays the glory of Christ, who is the image of God. For what we preach is not ourselves, but Jesus Christ as Lord, and ourselves as your servants for Jesus' sake. For God, who said, 'Let light shine out of darkness,' made his light shine in our hearts to give us the light of the knowledge of God's glory displayed in the face of Christ. But we have this treasure in jars of clay to show that this all-surpassing power is from God and not from us. We are hard pressed on every side, but not crushed; perplexed, but not in despair; persecuted, but not abandoned; struck down, but not destroyed. We always carry around in our body the death of Jesus, so that the life of Jesus may also be revealed in our body. For we who are alive are always being given over to death for Jesus' sake, so that his life may also be revealed in our mortal body. So then, death is at work in us, but life is at work in you.[142]

---

[142] 2 Corinthians 4:2-12.

This is the apostle Paul explaining that by his preaching the truth of the gospel, his words will be accepted by all right-thinking people; and if there are some who don't accept what he is saying, it is because they have been so blinded by the attractions of the world that they are unable to believe. Paul says this with absolute certainty, because his message is not about himself, but God. The message is that 'Jesus is Lord',[143] that Paul is a servant for Jesus' sake, and this truth cannot be overturned by anyone or anything.

God said, 'Let there be light,'[144] when the world began, so that the work of God could be seen in the darkness, and God is saying it again to us and to those who believe, so that His light will shine in us and show the power of Christ as we preach the truth and live out the Christian life. This light shines in us as it shines in Christ Himself.

Paul then introduces an analogy about 'jars of clay', so that believers will understand God's light in us is by God's efforts, not by our own. Family treasures in first-century Palestine were often hidden in clay jars for security reasons, as they were just ordinary household ornaments and thus did not earn much attention. Paul refers to the light as the treasure and uses the clay jars to describe the believers who have the light inside them. He sees himself as frail and unworthy, and everyone else the same. The contrast between the treasure and the jar is used to illustrate the difference between our poor and weak humanity and the complete sufficiency of God.

---

[143] Romans 10:9.
[144] Genesis 1:3.

When Paul writes about his carrying the death of Jesus, he is referring to his human weaknesses. He may list the hardships and persecutions he has suffered for preaching the gospel, but he is keen to say he is not overwhelmed. Paul is not complaining about his treatment, but sharing his experiences in order to forewarn, as well as encourage, other believers down the ages who will follow in his footsteps. By saying he carries the death of Jesus, it provides the background against which the life of Jesus can also be seen in him, and the power of Christ will be seen helping Paul to overcome the hardships.

There were many opponents to the gospel when Jesus walked on earth, but He gave His light to the world to counteract this. In this age, there are still many opponents to the gospel, so Jesus uses believers to shine His light for Him. In the Sermon on the Mount, Jesus affirms this when He tells us we are the 'salt of the earth' and the 'light of the world'.[145]

If we preach Jesus is Lord, those who are not blinded and deafened by the world will see and hear the truth. We may suffer hardship as Paul did, but our obvious frailty will ensure the listeners look to the treasure, and not at the jars.

Thoughts for reflection before we talk with God

Imagine you are travelling with the apostle Paul on one of his ministry journeys. You have seen Paul being totally dependent on Jesus as he travels from place to place. You have also seen him being stretched to his absolute limits.

---

[145] Matthew 5:13-16.

Paul is explaining to the people of Corinth that believers have to share the suffering of Jesus in order to 'know the power of his resurrection'.[146] Do you think you and Paul would make a good team?

Reflect upon the work you do today in your place of witness, mission or ministry. Perhaps you are suffering some of the hardships that Paul endured. Paul said he was 'hard pressed ... perplexed ... persecuted ... struck down', but not to the point of defeat. Paul found a way to use the strength of the Lord in his work. He also relied on his friends and co-workers. Do you feel crushed, despairing, abandoned or broken? Are you near burnout or collapse? Are you putting aside the time needed for you and Jesus to talk and plan together, and to spend time with family and/or friends, or does the serving sometimes encroach on the personal time, so that time for refreshment is postponed or cancelled?

Jesus is familiar with the pressures of a busy working life, since He worked in Joseph's carpentry shop for many years. After His return from the wilderness, His time in ministry was almost non-stop. Once He compared Himself to foxes and birds and said He had no place to rest.[147] Yet He did have a system to prevent overload, such as when He avoided towns and stayed out of sight of the crowds,[148] or when He got up early in the morning and went to a 'solitary place' to pray.[149] Jesus is familiar with church work, ministry work, secular work and the tug-of-

---

146 See 2 Corinthians 4:11; Philippians 3:10.
147 See Matthew 8:20.
148 See Mark 9:30.
149 Mark 1:35.

war between work and leisure time. Jesus knows how to help His workers avoid being struck down or destroyed; He wants all His workers to have a proper work–rest balance. He has already walked the paths where we walk.

Jesus is interested and involved in everything done in His name, and as He enjoyed time spent alone with His disciples, so He enjoys time spent talking with us. Why not discuss your working routines and see if there is overload in any area instead of balance? Or if you need to reset times to meet Him? You could look over recent events in your busy life and ask if He has provided you with a blessing or kindness you didn't recognise, or sent an angel with a message which you didn't give enough attention to. Perhaps ask Him for discernment for dealing with what's ahead.

The conversation

Imagine meeting Jesus for a conversation about your Christian work, in a place you associate with it, perhaps your workplace, a study, a vestry or the site of a current project. You're sitting together, although it might be a bit squashed. With the Spirit leading the way, why not start to talk with Jesus about the way God's light is shining in and through your life and ministry, and how to appropriate the power of Christ into your working routine, to provide you with strength and wisdom day by day.

A prayer to finish

Lord Jesus, thank You for partnering me in my work and witness. I do find it challenging sometimes, but I accept that I am asked to suffer some hardship so that I can reveal Your presence in my life when it matters.

Thank You that Your favour is always sufficient for me, and that Your power is at its strongest when I am at my weakest.[150]Teach me, please, not to strive on my own, but to accept the reality that it's Your light shining in me, and thus my work is a shared experience between You and me. Amen.

---

[150] See 2 Corinthians 12:9.

20
The Lord's Requirements

Listen to what the LORD says:
'Stand up, plead my case before the mountains;
let the hills hear what you have to say.
Hear, you mountains, the LORD's accusation;
listen, you everlasting foundations of the earth.
For the LORD has a case against his people;
he is lodging a charge against Israel.
My people, what have I done to you?
How have I burdened you? Answer me.
I brought you up out of Egypt
and redeemed you from the land of slavery.
I sent Moses to lead you,
also Aaron and Miriam.
My people, remember
what Balak king of Moab plotted
and what Balaam son of Beor answered.
Remember your journey from Shittim to Gilgal,
that you may know the righteous acts of the LORD.'
With what shall I come before the LORD
and bow down before the exalted God?
Shall I come before him with burnt offerings,
with calves a year old?
Will the LORD be pleased with thousands of rams,
with ten thousand rivers of oil?
Shall I offer my firstborn for my transgression,
the fruit of my body for the sin of my soul?

He has shown you, O mortal, what is good.
And what does the LORD require of you?
To act justly and to love mercy
and to walk humbly with your God.[151]

This passage has important guidance on how we are to live our Christian life and is set out as though a hearing is taking place in a court of law. God calls on His prophet to put forward His complaint, so Micah calls the mountains, the hills and the 'foundations of the earth' to listen as witnesses. God then speaks out the prosecution case; that despite all the good things He has done for the Israelites in the past, such as helping them escape from slavery in Egypt, or appointing people of integrity as their leaders, or heaping up the waters in the River Jordan so the people could cross over to the promised land with dry feet,[152] the people's attitude towards Him is no longer respectful, or in any way grateful.

The people defend themselves by claiming ignorance of what is required of them, asking God which type of sacrifice would please Him, and how much of it does He want? Reflecting on their response, which includes them offering 'ten thousand rivers of oil', or their children as ransom for their sins, their reply comes across as very cynical and tends to support the reality of the complaint that God is making.

Micah replies on behalf of God and makes two points. First, God has told the people previously that they need to show respect when talking to Him, for this is not a

---

[151] Micah 6:1-8.
[152] See Joshua 3:16.

conversation between equals – the people are mere mortals, living on the earth, whereas God is Spirit and the creator of all things; He has called them to be 'a kingdom of priests and a holy nation'[153] and He is entitled to, and worthy of, their respect.

Second, Micah speaks out what God is expecting from the new relationship which will exist between Himself and His people in future: for people to exhibit God's justice and mercy when interacting with other people, and to display true humility in all their dealings with Him. God is not seeking just a rehash of the old offerings originating in the past, from people who are bored and busy, but a sincere new relationship between Himself and His people, and between the people themselves, which demonstrates a desire and a heart to honour and respect each other.

'To act justly' includes speaking truthfully and making fair judgements; 'to love mercy' includes right and loving behaviour towards God and our neighbours; 'to walk humbly with … God' includes us giving up our plans and ambitions, accepting God's plans for our life, listening to Him and respecting who He is. God is calling His people into a new relationship with Him, and is making clear that the old ways are no longer acceptable.

Thoughts for reflection before we talk with God

The new relationship is built on the attitudes of the heart, so to make it work well, God's people need to self-examine regularly and see if they do honour and respect God in all their dealings. Christians often undertake self-

---

[153] Exodus 19:6.

examination for the purpose of confession and forgiveness, either prior to a church service where the minister or leader will give words of forgiveness and pardon, or in private confession, at home or elsewhere, to receive God's forgiveness through His Spirit. These actions and prayers bring believers back into a right relationship with God. However, it can be beneficial if we also examine our relationship with God against specific teaching like that in Micah 6:8 and see how we are doing in our Christian life in these particular areas.

The saying 'familiarity breeds contempt' is a truth that can have an impact on any area of life if we start to act out of habit, rather than respect. Then our offerings, or sacrifices, can become a bit mechanical and they will not be pleasing to God in the way they should be. Our offerings can be things we do, the payments we make to our church, to the needy or to charitable causes, or the way we relate to people day to day. We are all susceptible to habit to some extent.

It can also happen with our acts of service and worship, which originally start with honour and praise for God, but become in time more like duty than pleasure, so they end up being just the same old sacrifices, day after day, month after month, without any heart. If we allow our sacrifices to God to become stale, we don't please Him; we disappoint Him. God would much prefer small offerings from a loving, 'contrite heart'[154] than a magnificent offering given without respect or love. In the Sermon on

---

[154] Psalm 51:17.

the Mount, Jesus gave some advice about having the right heart before offering a gift to God.[155]

Speaking with God and discussing our Christian life as measured against Micah's guidelines might be seen as a kind of school report, or an audit. If the Spirit reveals there have been times in the past when justice was not served, or mercy was withheld, or humility was absent, we can respond by taking the opportunity to sort it out immediately: we could admit our errors, say we're sorry, receive our forgiveness and move on in life. Such conversations restore our freedom and give us peace.

Why not have a conversation with Jesus about this? You could tell Him what you have been doing for God and His kingdom, about your times of worship and praise, or your service to others, be they at home, in the community, in church, in the workplace or serving your country. You could ask Him if His standards of justice, mercy and humility have been met in the working-out. Perhaps there are things that you would admit have not been as righteous as you had intended or hoped. Perhaps our sacrifices have become a bit stale over the weeks and months and years.

The conversation

Imagine you're meeting with Jesus to talk about how you're doing in your Christian life. You are in a beautiful location, sitting together, with a range of hills and mountains nearby. As you rest in the Spirit, and taking His lead, let Him help you ask Jesus if there are areas in your life where He desires to deepen your understanding of

---

[155] See Matthew 5:23-24.

what He is asking from you in regard to justice and mercy and humility, and so learn a gentler way to live.

A prayer to finish

Father, thank You that I can come into Your presence and talk about how I am faring in my walk with You. Thank You that although some of my efforts to honour and respect You are less than perfect, You are quick to forgive and encourage me to try again.

I pray that, with more practice, I will become more like the person You want me to be, and that I will reflect Your character wherever I go. Amen.

21
My Times Are in Your Hands

Be merciful to me, LORD, for I am in distress;
my eyes grow weak with sorrow,
my soul and body with grief.
My life is consumed by anguish
and my years by groaning;
my strength fails because of my affliction,
and my bones grow weak.
Because of all my enemies,
I am the utter contempt of my neighbours
and an object of dread to my closest friends –
those who see me on the street flee from me.
I am forgotten as though I were dead;
I have become like broken pottery.
For I hear many whispering,
'Terror on every side!'
They conspire against me
and plot to take my life.
But I trust in you, LORD;
I say, 'You are my God.'
My times are in your hands;
deliver me from the hands of my enemies,
from those who pursue me.
Let your face shine on your servant;
save me in your unfailing love.
Let me not be put to shame, LORD,
for I have cried out to you;

> *but let the wicked be put to shame*
> *and be silent in the realm of the dead.*
> *Let their lying lips be silenced,*
> *for with pride and contempt*
> *they speak arrogantly against the righteous.*[156]

This psalm is a prayer of David for deliverance from his enemies. He cries out at a time when he is exhausted physically, emotionally and spiritually, in fear of death, abandoned, and seeing 'terror on every side'. The psalm starts with strong declarations about the Lord being his 'rock and ... fortress' in verse 3 and David having his feet set in a 'spacious place' in verse 8, but come verse 9 we read about the depth of his pit and the darkness of his mood. Yet just a few verses later, there is another change. The list of woe has ended and David's equilibrium is restored. First he admits 'I trust in you, LORD; I say "You are my God"', then he humbly accepts his situation and is able to say to God, 'My times are in your hands.'

This psalm is a good illustration of how emotion can undermine faith, while facts can restore the situation. Is there a touch of self-pity when David lists how bleak his future looks? In a similar situation, perhaps most of us would be in the same state. If we are held captive by emotion, it becomes hard to keep seeing God beside us, but when we stand on the facts alone, sight can return. By declaring he trusts in his Lord and that God is his God, David is able to see that God has sovereignty over all his times – good times, bad times, tough times, even the darkest of times.

---

[156] Psalm 31:9-18.

Even if David loses sight of God in his fear and pain, God never loses sight of David. So, using this knowledge, David's faith can fight back, and he looks to God in faith and speaks out in faith. He is able to ask God for future blessings, seek protection from his enemies and declare how great is the goodness of the Lord. In the power of the Spirit, we can do this too.

Thoughts for reflection before we talk with God

Psalm 31 is a good example of what happens when emotion causes blindness to the truth. David had a strong faith and trust in God, but in the depth of his fear and pain, he lost sight of Him. Only by reverting to the bedrock of his being, his knowledge that he trusted the Lord, that God is faithful, and that there was a strong personal relationship between them, did David recover his understanding of God's constant presence in good times and bad.

Has there been a time when you suffered so much pain or despair that you lost sight of God, or couldn't hear His voice? Perhaps you felt abandoned by Him, maybe even in fear of death? David knew the best and worst of times and wrote about them, and we can take strength from his experiences. He praised God for being his refuge and his fortress, even while he was suffering, and in doing that he got his priorities right. He praised God for His goodness before he listed all the things that were causing him grief. He praised Him for His faithfulness, because he knew God would not make a promise that He wouldn't keep. He knew he had not been handed over to the enemy, even though he was left by his friends and he had no army to defend him. He knew God stored up goodness for those who feared Him and took refuge in Him, and David waited expectantly to receive that goodness.

If we find ourselves in circumstances similar in gravity to those David experienced, we too can make a declaration like David did, that all our times are in God's hands. Speaking out a declaration builds up our faith. After that, we can look back on our life and see when and where God was active in our good times; what He did, what He arranged, what He changed, what blessings were suddenly available to us. Then we can look back to the times when we were in trouble and see where God was active in our bad times; what He did, what He arranged, what He changed, and all the rest. We do this to regain our perspective; we stand on the facts.

Knowing God's presence in our good times is a happy experience. Not finding God in our bad times can be a lonely experience; we can feel isolated, even if there is company nearby, and we can feel powerless, in that we feel we cannot change our situation. But feelings are not reliable. Imagine Jesus coming to meet you in your place of refuge, the place you retreat to when times are tough, and Him sitting beside you. You may feel no one can relate to you, that your friends and family cannot comprehend your despair, but Jesus will understand. He will stay with you until the facts overpower the feelings. You may wonder why God lets you suffer, or doesn't answer your prayers; sometimes we have to wait for God's reply, but He will reveal everything in His perfect time.

When you start to talk with Jesus, you could talk about the trials and tribulations of life generally. You could ask Him why life has so many bad times, so much pain, with seemingly so little relief at times. Some of our friends can be quick to share their opinion why, but asking Jesus is much better. You could ask Him why some people seem to skip though life without appearing to have much trouble at all, while others seem to be subjected continuously to stress of one kind or another; or you could ask why there was no answer to your cry for help when you were in distress, or consumed with grief. You could ask Him to help you speak out in faith when you feel incapable of doing so. If you ask the Spirit to lead you, He will help you with the question to start your talk with Jesus.

The conversation

Imagine Jesus still sitting beside you in your place of refuge. Maybe it takes you a while to recognise His presence, but now your heart warms and you're feeling safe. Imagine the two of you sharing something to eat and drink, taking in sustenance. It's time to talk, so as you look to start the conversation, resting in the Spirit, maybe you could ask Jesus to affirm again that He is Sovereign over the lives of all His people forever, even in the hard times when doubts seek to undermine faith, and then ask the Spirit to apply His words to your situation.

A prayer to finish

Dear Lord, thank You that You exercise Your sovereign will over my life. Help me to accept that Your timing is always perfect and that for me to experience bad times is not a punishment, nor a sign of Your displeasure, but an opportunity to help me develop the qualities You desire in me for service in Your kingdom.

I know that I can trust You in all things. Give me strength to persevere in my hardships, please. I know You are faithful; thank You for Your constant love. Amen.

22
Forget the Former Things

This is what the LORD says —
he who made a way through the sea,
a path through the mighty waters,
who drew out the chariots and horses,
the army and reinforcements together,
and they lay there, never to rise again,
extinguished, snuffed out like a wick:
'Forget the former things;
do not dwell on the past.
See, I am doing a new thing!
Now it springs up; do you not perceive it?
I am making a way in the wilderness
and streams in the wasteland.'[157]

This passage is about moving on and looking ahead. God is telling His people to avoid focusing on yesterday's victories and living in the past, because it hinders the view of the future. God does 'great and awesome deeds'.[158] The escape of the people of Israel from their captivity in Egypt was so amazing that it is no wonder the people can't stop thinking about their deliverance. Yet God says, 'Forget it.'

---

[157] Isaiah 43:16-19.
[158] Deuteronomy 4:34.

Why is that? Because God is telling them He is going to do more 'great and awesome' things in the future – and He needs them to be looking in the right direction to see them.

The same principle applies to us today. We have had blessings in the past, but God wants us to look for the new things He has planned for us.

A wilderness is an area of land that hasn't been inhabited or cultivated and can be a scary and lonely place; the lack of a visible way can make it a forlorn experience. Once there is evidence of a path or road, hope rises and there is an expectation of safe arrival at a destination. Wastelands are areas that have been inhabited and cultivated, but are now empty because the resources have been exhausted or the land is no longer usable. Once new streams flow, there will be new life and new growth, and fresh opportunities will be uncovered. This is what God promises to do for us when He is the guide in our lives.

Jesus also talked about new things coming to replace the old. Jesus counselled against pouring 'new wine into old wineskins'[159] in case the old skin failed and the wine was lost. His message resonates with the verse in Isaiah – there is a time to put aside past things and to take up the new thing that God is going to do in our lives. New wine is a blessing for its own time, but it can be lost if it's still reliant in some way on the old things of the past.

Thoughts for reflection before we talk with God

God wants us to grow and mature as we get older. If we stay still and get too comfortable, we are in danger of

---

[159] Matthew 9:17.

stagnation; inaction can lead to apathy if we're not careful. God's instruction to His people Israel to 'forget the former things' and let go of the past is quickly followed by His saying He's 'doing a new thing', that it is happening now, and can they recognise it? Then He tells them the plan – He's making a new way in one place and starting new streams in another. So, if we are serious with God and intend to 'forget the former things', our priority is to look for the 'new thing', which will be visible to a discerning eye and will be for our benefit and blessing. This is God being generous, wanting the best for us.

If we want reassurance that God's 'new thing' will be good, we can look back to the past and see His previous good gifts. Do you remember some of the more significant changes that have occurred in your past? What happened when God revealed a new opportunity for you? Perhaps it was in a wilderness – an opening in a new area of life that you didn't know about, until suddenly there was a visible way through it – or in a wasteland, where a good time in your life, which you thought had run its course, suddenly sprang back to life because 'a new stream' started flowing. One or two examples may come to mind if you rest and ponder, for God has been active in your life. As you recognise these good things, you could give a word of thanks to the Lord.

Looking on the reverse, maybe think about past opportunities that you did not take up, where you are standing still in some aspect of your life, wondering with hindsight if you missed something new God had planned for you, the things you didn't perceive. If you have regrets about opportunities that slipped away, it would be healing to give those regrets to God and be released from them, for they are not helpful for the future. Jesus will help you do this if you ask Him.

Consider when God last did a 'new thing' for you. If it's recent, brilliant! If it's a long time ago, you might ask Him what keeps you from seeing the new things, or from taking hold of what God has planned for you. If you think it could be hurts and failures from the past, or successes on which you have rested for too long, or perhaps a fear of what may lie ahead, this would be a good time to talk to God. The Holy Spirit will help you sift through your memories.

There is much we can discuss with Jesus when we have a conversation about moving on. We could ask Him to show us the times where we did embrace new things, and the blessings that have flowed from them, even if we were too involved to notice; and to show us what has hindered our move into other freedom spaces He wants us to enjoy. We could ask for help to forget former things that keep us from moving on, and to identify things in the past we could let go of, so as to make room for new things. Letting go might relate to possessions, souvenirs, paper records, habits, extra responsibilities, things we've always done and all kinds of other things that have outlived their season. Sometimes our lives can become so clogged with stuff that we compromise our ability to think with clarity, to see clearly or to make decisions. Why not ask the Holy Spirit to act as your guide as you pray about your future?

The conversation

Imagine meeting Jesus in a desert wasteland, where the terrain is harsh, the natural resources have been used, and it's empty because it has no further use. As you stand there together, looking around, with the Spirit reminding you how God can use fresh water to renew the dry times in our lives, why not ask the Spirit to guide you into a conversation with Jesus about the opportunities He gives for moving on, and for letting go of the past.

A prayer to finish

Lord, Your Word tells us that You are 'the gate for the sheep', that 'They will come in and go out, and find pasture'; and that You have come so the sheep can 'have life, and have it to the full'.[160] *Often that means taking hold of the future and letting go of things in the past.*

Please would You heal the bad memories in my past, so I can let them go; and help me learn from the good experiences of my life, so I am better equipped for the future. I want to live my future life to the full, but I can only do this with You involved.

Please would You help me to walk in faith, and see the new things You are providing for me. Life is so much better when I keep within Your plan. Thank You. Amen.

---

[160] John 10:7-10.

23
Be Holy

Therefore, with minds that are alert and fully sober, set your hope on the grace to be brought to you when Jesus Christ is revealed at his coming. As obedient children, do not conform to the evil desires you had when you lived in ignorance. But just as he who called you is holy, so be holy in all you do; for it is written: 'Be holy, because I am holy.'[161]

In his letter to Christians in Asia Minor, the apostle Peter is encouraging the believers to be holy. Peter spent three years with Jesus during His ministry and he knows true holiness can be achieved, because Jesus was the perfect example; yet, being realistic, for the rest of humanity, being holy is a real challenge.

Holiness is being totally free from sin, and God is and always has been that. The instruction to be holy was first given to Moses by God when the people of Israel were camped at Mount Sinai and Moses was being told of God's plan. If they obeyed God and kept His covenant, then they would be His 'treasured possession ... a kingdom of priests and a holy nation'.[162] God's offer was unanimously

---

[161] 1 Peter 1:13-16.
[162] Exodus 19:5-6.

accepted and holiness became a benchmark for the relationship. God had told the people clearly He was holy and that they needed to imitate His holiness to the best of their ability – to be holy because He was holy – otherwise the agreement wouldn't work. This would require of them wisdom, discernment and a commitment to the practical consequence of the agreement – they would have to separate themselves from the unholy activities of the world.

Writing to the people of Rome after the resurrection, the apostle Paul explains how people are changed by accepting Jesus as their Lord. Before grace takes effect, Paul describes the people as being 'slaves to sin', but after believers meet Jesus and follow Him, they are set free from sin and become 'slaves to righteousness' instead.[163] With Jesus, no one is a slave to anything, but the term describes the right level of commitment. Living out the gospel does produce holiness and prepares us for eternal life.

Conversely, those who do not seek holiness, nor have a desire for Jesus, will not obtain eternal life with God, unless there is a change of heart and a plea to the Spirit for help.

Holiness should be visible in the lives of those who commit to following Jesus. This is because the purpose of our life on earth is to get ourselves ready to live in the next world, and to learn about obedience, justice, righteousness, moderation, steadfastness and many other qualities, because these are what we will find there. The Holy Spirit teaches us these qualities as He dwells within us and we practise what we learn.

---

[163] Romans 6:16,18.

Unfortunately, it is not easy to be holy on earth. Paul admitted openly he didn't understand himself. When he decided to do something good, often he found himself distracted before the job was done, and when he tried to avoid doing something he knew was harmful, he often ended up doing it anyway. Such contrary behaviour became a great source of frustration for him and he criticised himself harshly for his own weakness, asking who could rescue him from his desperate situation. Then, with the help of the Holy Spirit, he saw the answer to his own question and declared Jesus would be His rescuer.[164]

If we find ourselves in the same situation and ask who will rescue us, we will get the same answer. It is Jesus who saves us too.

Thoughts for reflection before we talk with God

Imagine yourself being one of the disciples travelling with Jesus through Judea and around Galilee and observing the dynamics of the group. You can see how they live and interact with each other. You see how Jesus spent so much time in prayer with the Father, often going to out-of-the-way places; how He thought before He spoke; how He was precise and polite in His language, especially when talking with those who criticised Him or tried to catch Him out. You can see how the disciples tried to imitate Jesus, and the times when they failed, such as when they argued about who was 'the greatest', or when some tried to reserve the best seats in heaven.[165]

---

[164] See Romans 7:15-19; 24-25.
[165] Mark 9:34; 10:35-37.

Life in the world today does not encourage holiness. It can be revealing if we ask ourselves what we look at, what we read, what we become exposed to from choices on the internet and television. We could ask if our conversation is honouring to God and respectful of others.

Do we need to be more discerning about what we take in? We are made up of body, mind and spirit and each component is affected by what we absorb. What we eat and drink, if bad or in excess, can make us ill physically; some of the material we look at and listen to may harm us mentally and emotionally; becoming involved in spiritual activities that are in opposition to God's Word will make us ill spiritually. All of these things can affect how we speak, think and act. Is there anything in our lifestyle that has a form of control over us?

Why not take some time to consider your lifestyle? Living a holy life is a challenge that presents itself every day, but we are never on our own, for the Holy Spirit lives in us to help and guide us. Jesus knows we reflect the world more than we reflect Him – but His grace is always available; if we fall down, He will pick us up.

A conversation with Jesus about holiness will be helpful. The subject may not be at the top of our agenda, for there are so many other qualities to aim for, but holiness is an indication of how much we love and respect God, and the Holy Spirit will be helping us as we move towards being more holy. And as we seek to grow in holiness, we can rest secure in the knowledge that any shortfall is made up by Jesus, because He is our righteousness and our holiness.[166]

---

[166] See 1 Corinthians 1:30.

The conversation

Revisit the scene where you imagine being a disciple travelling through Judea and Galilee with Jesus and the disciples. They have stopped for the night, the evening meal has been shared, and you see Jesus on His own. As you mull over whether to approach Him, He turns round and looks at you and beckons you to come nearer, showing you where to sit. And as you consider talking to Him about holiness, perhaps you could ask the Spirit to show you some part of your life where you might make a start towards living more like the way Jesus lived, and then follow the Spirit as He leads you into a deeper union.

A prayer to finish

Father God, You instruct Your people to consecrate themselves, and to be holy, because You are holy. I want this too, and I will seek Your face in this desire.

Help me, please, to separate myself from the distractions of the world and to dedicate myself to Your priorities. I know You love the things I do for You, but I realise holiness grows better in the quality time I spend in Your presence, just being with You, rather than in the time I spend doing things for You.

It is only with holiness that I will see You more clearly. Teach me, Lord, how to be holy. Amen.

24
Follow Me

The third time he said to him, 'Simon son of John, do you love me?'
Peter was hurt because Jesus asked him the third time, 'Do you love me?' He said, 'Lord, you know all things; you know that I love you.' ...
Jesus said this to indicate the kind of death by which Peter would glorify God. Then he said to him, 'Follow me!'
Peter turned and saw that the disciple whom Jesus loved was following them. (This was the one who had leaned back against Jesus at the supper and had said, 'Lord, who is going to betray you?') When Peter saw him, he asked, 'Lord, what about him?'
Jesus answered, 'If I want him to remain alive until I return, what is that to you? You must follow me.' Because of this, the rumour spread among the believers that this disciple would not die. But Jesus did not say that he would not die; he only said, 'If I want him to remain alive until I return, what is that to you?'[167]

The above passage is the latter part of a conversation Jesus and Peter had in Galilee, sometime after the resurrection. Peter and the disciples had met the risen Jesus in Jerusalem on the day of the resurrection and a joyful

---

[167] John 21:17,19-23.

reunion had taken place, repeated a week later with Thomas now present, but one would suppose Peter would still be weighed down with embarrassment and shame following his denials on the night before the crucifixion. After the second meeting, Peter and some of the disciples had returned to Galilee, where the fishermen could resume their old livelihoods.

On one fishing trip, when they had fished all night without success, Jesus appeared on the shore in the morning and asked if they had any fish. Being told they hadn't, He suggested where they should cast their net and, having done so, they made an enormous catch. Such a result prompted closer inspection of the figure on the shore, and after Jesus was recognised, Peter swam ashore immediately, while the boat with the catch followed.

When they landed, Jesus invited the disciples to bring some of their catch to cook and to eat breakfast with Him, and when the meal was ready, He handed out the bread and the fish, just as He had done during His ministry. Such a small gesture, and yet such a treasure, for it would have reminded the disciples of their past times together, while affirming again the reality of His resurrection.

After the meal was finished, imagine Jesus and Peter having a walk for a private conversation. We are told only a part of what was said, but we can surmise that Jesus would have spoken directly into Peter's three denials[168] and the shame that still held him. Jesus asked Peter three times if he loved Him, and with Peter's affirmative answers, Jesus restored and healed him, telling him three

---

[168] See for example Matthew 26:69-75. Verse 34 tells us that Jesus knew Peter would deny Him.

times to care for His flock, and warning him that the manner of his death would bring glory to God. He ended by telling Peter to follow Him, which were words He had used when He first called Peter to join Him.[169] Peter would have understood the past was now dealt with, and a new future beckoned.

At this point, Peter turned around and saw John following them, so he asked, 'Lord, what about him?' Jesus acknowledged Peter's question with a different question, and then repeated His instruction to Peter, but with greater emphasis: 'You must follow me.'

We can learn from this conversation. First, all of us are capable of denying Jesus, and most of us would admit to having done so on occasion, but denying Jesus is not unforgiveable. Forgiveness and reinstatement are available to us in the same way it was given to Peter. Sometimes there may be a time of waiting, until Jesus counts us ready. The time spent fishing in Galilee gave Peter the time and space for the healing of his wounded heart, to get a truthful perspective on what had happened, and to be open to taking back his calling. Jesus knew the demands and trials that lay ahead for Peter, so He gave him advice that was clear and unambiguous: 'You must follow me.' We should hear this too, if we stumble and are reinstated by God. Reinstatement removes the stains of the past and reignites the desire to serve.

Second, part of that private conversation led to a false rumour, which John felt he had to correct. How did that start? Possibly a lesson here is that we should refrain from concerning ourselves with someone else's calling and

---

[169] See Matthew 4:18-19.

keep ourselves firmly focused on our own. Jesus will tell us all we need to know when it comes to another's calling.

Thoughts for reflection before we talk with God

Has there been a time in your life when you stumbled and felt shame, embarrassment and failure? Feeling you had let God down when you were confident you would stand firm, and now you're trying to repair the damage? Sometimes the feelings lessen in intensity as time passes, but still we may be seeking forgiveness and reinstatement to restore our personal relationship with God. Or perhaps we are suffering such emotions now, praying to recover what we have lost.

It was likely a difficult conversation that Peter had with Jesus on the beach, for we read in verse 17 that Peter was 'hurt' by the third question; yet he persevered, because he knew reconciliation with Jesus would be reward enough. Peter may have asked Jesus some questions, such as could He not have saved him from that awful situation? Perhaps he questioned why Jesus stuck with him when he had shown himself to be so unreliable. You could ask Jesus these questions too if they speak to you, or perhaps you have your own difficult questions if there's something you need to settle with Jesus. All of us have our difficult times, but talking with Jesus brings everything into the open.

The story of Peter is very encouraging. Here is a man who says the wrong things, speaks before thinking, follows his heart to the point where he can embarrass himself in front of others, overpromises what he will do, falls asleep when he shouldn't and lets his best friend down.[170] Yet Jesus loved him so much that He took him into the house when He healed the young girl, took him up the mountain when He met Elijah and Moses and heard His Father speak, called him to walk on the water, and reinstated him so he became the first among equals when it came to building the Church.[171]

Do you ever think you don't fit in, or that your skills are not appreciated? Maybe that your mission and ministry work don't count for much? Do you feel that you're unreliable? Don't you believe any of it! Look at Peter's story. Each of us has unique skills and God uses us uniquely. It's all about heart. If we talk with Jesus, He will tell us He chooses us for who we are! He will explain what He wants us to do. Peter resumed his leadership position with the disciples, and Jesus will give us new opportunities for the future.

The conversation

Imagine yourself on a pebbly beach, clear sky, sunny day, talking with Jesus. You've just shared breakfast, chatting about inconsequential things, and now you're walking together, just the two of you. How will you open the conversation you're longing for, the one that enables you to start again with a clean sheet? Do you want to make an apology – is that a place to start? Or perhaps an explanation? If you listen to the Spirit, He will guide you on what to say first, and then He'll walk with you towards complete forgiveness and healing.

---

[170] See Mark 9:5-6; Matthew 16:22; Luke 5:8; Matthew 26:35,40,69-75.
[171] See Mark 5:37-42: Mark 9:2-7; Matthew 14:29; John 21; Acts 2:14.

A prayer to finish

Lord Jesus, I thank You that when I stumble in a bad way, You meet me in my pain and loss and share the journey back to forgiveness and reinstatement. You seek my assurances that I love You: Lord, You know that I do.

Equip me and teach me the right way to follow You, I pray. Thank You that by Your grace, You call me again to serve You. May I be more like You as I seek to live out my calling. Amen.

25
Walking in the Light

This is the message we have heard from him and declare to you: God is light; in him there is no darkness at all. If we claim to have fellowship with him and yet walk in the darkness, we lie and do not live out the truth. But if we walk in the light, as he is in the light, we have fellowship with one another, and the blood of Jesus, his Son, purifies us from all sin.
If we claim to be without sin, we deceive ourselves and the truth is not in us. If we confess our sins, he is faithful and just and will forgive us our sins and purify us from all unrighteousness.[172]

This is the apostle John telling us how God describes Himself: 'God is light' and He excludes anything and everything that is not light. Light symbolises what is good, true and holy, while darkness represents what is not good, false or unholy.

Walking in the darkness and walking in the light describe two opposing lifestyles – one characterised by rebellion to God's way, the other by following God's laws and living by the truth. Things done in the light can be seen and do not cause fear because there is nothing to hide.

---

[172] 1 John 1:5-9.

Things opposed to God's way are often done in the darkness and demand secrecy because they cannot bear unrestricted scrutiny and carry a fear of discovery.

To have fellowship with Christ is to live in a spiritual union with God. The passage underscores the truth about sin; to deny that sin exists, or that we can be guilty of it, is to 'deceive ourselves'. No one is righteous, not a single person,[173] yet all is not lost; for God showed His love for us, and Jesus died for us 'while we were ... sinners'.[174] If we will admit that we do sin, and confess the sin before God, then God fulfils His promise and forgives us, making us pure again.

Our natural inclination is to shy away from our mistakes and offences, to hide from them, ignore them or blot them out of our mind. We see no problem with little white lies, or with being economical with the truth when it suits us, or when we think the end result justifies whatever means we use to achieve it.

To give evidence in a court of law, witnesses are required to swear they will tell 'the truth, the whole truth, and nothing but the truth'. 'The truth' in this context sets out the threshold required: 'the whole truth' demands that nothing should be omitted so as to give only part of the story, which means we can't leave out the bits that don't help us, or don't show us in a good light; and 'nothing but the truth' demands that untrue and misleading information cannot be added to the evidence so as to blur the truth, or misdirect the judge and jury.

---

[173] See Romans 3:10.
[174] Romans 5:8.

Walking in the light may ask a great deal of those who seek to walk with Jesus, but it also brings the greatest reward. Confession and repentance is the only way to forgiveness and regaining our freedom. If we confess our sins, we are released from all the shame, guilt and fear of punishment that comes as a result of sin and we can live in the security, lightness of spirit and freedom that Jesus promises.

Thoughts for reflection before we talk with God

Can you imagine walking in light which is really dazzlingly bright, yet unexpectedly soft and totally pain-free to your eyes? This is what walking with Jesus will be like in the perfect world – we will be completely at ease and very comfortable. Sadly, this world is not perfect, and thus for us, walking in the light each day is not an easy task. Even though Jesus is truth and light and His Spirit is present in the world, there is much conflict between light and darkness, and truth and untruth, which makes our life very challenging. But since walking in the light is an important part of Christian living, to talk about it with Jesus can help us greatly in our efforts to be successful.

It is a tough battle between light and darkness, truth and untruth, because both sides want to claim our loyalty. Why not ask Jesus to show us any areas in our life where we may be leaving an opening for the enemy to interfere? Sometimes the darkness masquerades as light and it is not easy to identify. Perhaps we could ask Jesus about the people we share our time with, at work or at leisure; are they people who truly share our desire to walk in the light, or might they be people who walk in the dark and seek to lead us astray? Or we could ask if all the places we frequent belong to the light, or if any are not what they appear to be. Are there any activities that hinder our walking in the good way, or new ideas to be adopted that would assist life in the light?

Walking in the light also affects our attitude to authority. The apostle Paul advised believers about submitting to the governing authorities, because worldly authorities have been set up by God for the benefit of those who live in community.[175] Those in authority are under God too, and will not be a cause of worry or concern to those who act correctly, whereas any of us who rebel against authorities instituted by God are warned that judgement may come upon us. Do the actions taken by governments, or by those in any level of authority, or some of their decisions, cause us to be uneasy in our spirit or conscience? We can ask Jesus to explain His way and guide us in our future relationships with authority. If you have a specific complaint even now, why not take it to Jesus?

If the Holy Spirit is restless within us, He may be warning us that we have wandered away from the good path on occasion, or walked outside the light. If this is the case, we can bring these times to Jesus, because God will forgive us. Mistakes and sins that are forgiven lose their power to make us afraid, or to make us feel guilty or ashamed. They have no further hold on us. As we talk with Jesus, we can share our hopes and the desires of our heart and ask His guiding Spirit to lead us, both in the walking and in the protection we need along the way.

---

[175] See Romans 13:1-7.

The conversation

Imagine meeting Jesus on a lovely bright day, when the sky is blue and the air is cool, perhaps in a favourite garden, or on a beach or mountaintop. It's like one of those meetings that are not planned, but happen through a lovely coincidence; you blink, and there He is – beside you! So, basking in the presence of Jesus, why not let the Spirit guide you into talking with Jesus about the freedoms to be enjoyed while walking in the light, compared with the deceits and dangers of living in the darkness, and about the skills to learn in order to avoid drifting away from the light.

A prayer to finish

Father God, I do not fully understand Your great love, but fortunately I do not need to. My eternal future rests on the promises of Jesus, who has already bought my freedom. Although I live in this world, I have been raised with Jesus for life eternal with You, so please would You help me focus on the things of heaven? Yet, while I live here on earth, please guide me to walk in the good way, and to display 'the fruit of the Spirit'[176] as I journey, so that I can be seen as one who walks in the light, with You; and may I give credit for this to You alone. Thank You so much. Amen.

---

[176] Galatians 5:22-23.

26
Do Not Fret

Do not fret because of those who are evil
or be envious of those who do wrong;
for like the grass they will soon wither,
like green plants they will soon die away.
Trust in the LORD and do good;
dwell in the land and enjoy safe pasture.
Take delight in the LORD,
and he will give you the desires of your heart.
Commit your way to the LORD;
trust in him and he will do this:
he will make your righteous reward shine like the dawn,
your vindication like the noonday sun.
Be still before the LORD
and wait patiently for him;
do not fret when people succeed in their ways,
when they carry out their wicked schemes.
Refrain from anger and turn from wrath;
do not fret – it leads only to evil.
For those who are evil will be destroyed,
but those who hope in the LORD will inherit the land.[177]

This psalm of David contains good advice for those of us
who get anxious about what is happening in the world.

---

[177] Psalm 37:1-9

The reporting of news across the globe is now a twenty-four-hour business and the media is full of stories of scams, misfortunes, prejudice and all kinds of evil. Everyone seems to have a view, and the way those views are expressed can be aggressive, unfeeling and intolerant of anyone else's viewpoints.

With news accessible on demand on mobile phones and many other devices, and reported in a way that leaves us thinking we need more information quickly, we can fall into a mindset that makes us keep checking and reading, whereas we rarely need to know these things in a hurry. Much of the news is really depressing, and frequent exposure to bad news can lead to a feeling of despondency, especially if our views are biblically based and the views expressed in public appear to contravene God's law as we understand it. Sometimes a sense of unfairness can surface when we let ourselves think or feel that people who don't believe in God do better, get richer and have more comfortable lives than those who do believe, without all the delays and difficulties that law-abiding people often tend to suffer.[178]

The psalmist's advice is not to be concerned, because wisdom gives us the truth. God is our Maker, God sets out how we should live; 'Trust in the LORD' and keep doing the right thing. As we take pleasure in pleasing the Lord, committing our plans and actions to Him, He will guarantee we will not miss out on the good things He has in store for us. Not only that, His timing will be perfect and blessings will come in the right order.

---

[178] See Psalm 73.

Living contentedly in the world is challenging sometimes, but it helps if we can keep a true perspective in sight. Believers in Jesus live in the eternal world even while we live on earth. Jesus said that anyone who listens to Him, and believes God, 'has eternal life and will not be judged but has crossed over from death to life'.[179] We live in a world that has been saved by the death and resurrection of Jesus Christ. Eternal life with God starts for believers on earth, right now; it doesn't start in heaven, it continues in heaven.

So the alternative to fretting is to let the Spirit guide our thoughts each day; not being envious of those who seem to get away with doing the wrong thing, and not being angry when people succeed using unethical or unlawful ways, because these feelings will lead us into trouble. In due time, God will meet the people who live their life without regard to Him or His ways of living, and will work it out with them personally. For those who believe, our best interests are met if we will be quiet and worshipful before the Lord, and 'wait patiently' for Him. In this way, we acknowledge His lordship over our lives and can surrender our feelings, judgements and future ambitions to Him, and in return, as people who hope in the Lord, we will inherit all that God has promised.

Thoughts for reflection before we talk with God

Consider how you are feeling these days. Are you anxious, scared or fearful? Feelings are notoriously unreliable, but we are all affected by the events and circumstances of our daily lives, and feelings can sometimes make truth hard to

---

[179] John 5:24.

see. Bringing our feelings into the presence of God can change our lives, because the truth will overcome the deceptiveness of feelings and bring peace. A way to bring the events or situations that cause us unease into God's presence is, first, to make a list of them – situations, people, relationships, world events, whatever worries us – and, second, to give them to Jesus at the cross. It doesn't matter how small or silly the anxiety may seem, or how impossible or big the task; if you're upset by it, add it to the list – God can handle all of it.

Consider these two women in the Gospels: Martha had a domestic issue and brought her feelings of being left to do all the work to Jesus when He came to her home for a meal.[180] Or the woman who came to Jesus while He dined at the house of Simon the Pharisee.[181] She showed Jesus how she felt about herself, and Him, when she brought a jar of perfume and washed His feet and anointed them. Her issue was self-esteem and sin, but Jesus can deal with feelings, and both women were healed by their meetings with Him.

As we talk with Jesus, He will deal with each item on our list, bringing healing and peace. The old feelings we can put at the foot of the empty cross, and watch them fade away. It is the Lord who takes our burdens off us and we can walk into the future with freedom. You are God's precious child, we all are, and He wants the best for us.

Without the weight of constant anxiety caused by the things that worry us, emanating from feelings rather than facts, we can live the life of freedom that Jesus died to give

---

[180] See Luke 10:40.
[181] See Luke 7:37-38.

us. And these things can be taken to Jesus and left at the empty cross as often as you need to in the future.

The conversation

Imagine you are meeting Jesus at the empty cross. The aura is different, the darkness has gone, Jesus is risen, His victory is complete. He looks as you would imagine He looked when He appeared to the disciples on the first evening, and He offers you His peace, as He did to them. So, as you see yourself handing Jesus your list, allow the Spirit to guide you in what you say, and which item you mention first, and then with the next, and so on until it's all done.

A prayer to finish

Lord Jesus, You invite all those who are 'weary and burdened' to come to You so that You can give us rest. Thank You for Your love and Your offer to help. You instruct me to take Your yoke and learn from You, for You are 'gentle and humble in heart' and I will find total rest in You. I hear You say, 'My yoke is easy and my burden is light.' I know it in my head, but please teach me to know this in my heart also.[182]

Lord, please would You counsel me in future on which responsibilities and good causes I can sensibly take up and travel with

---

[182] Matthew 11:28-30.

safely, and which are the ones better left behind. Then I will avoid being weighed down by the things of the world, and carry only those things that display the hallmark of the Spirit. In Your precious name I pray. Amen.

27
Why We're Here

I keep asking that the God of our Lord Jesus Christ, the glorious Father, may give you the Spirit of wisdom and revelation, so that you may know him better. I pray that the eyes of your heart may be enlightened in order that you may know the hope to which he has called you, the riches of his glorious inheritance in his holy people, and his incomparably great power for us who believe. That power is the same as the mighty strength he exerted when he raised Christ from the dead and seated him at his right hand in the heavenly realms, far above all rule and authority, power and dominion, and every name that is invoked, not only in the present age but also in the one to come. And God placed all things under his feet and appointed him to be head over everything for the church, which is his body, the fullness of him who fills everything in every way.[183]

The apostle Paul's letter to the Ephesians was written to encourage and educate the young church in Ephesus, and tells us the reason why the world was created. In short, God's desire and purpose, which pre-dates the creation of the world, is to create a loving, holy and godly family for Himself, by choosing people from all nations of the earth

---

[183] Ephesians 1:17-23.

and adopting them as His children, through Jesus; and this is solely because it pleases Him.[184]

God's plan is achieved because, in Jesus, by grace, we have been redeemed through His death and forgiven our sins. At a time of God's choosing, the world will come to an end and the conclusion will be to unify everything in heaven and on earth under one person, Jesus Christ.[185] All the people on earth who believe in Jesus are saved, and are sealed with the presence of the Holy Spirit, who is the guarantee of our salvation until the end of the world, when Jesus returns to rule His kingdom.[186]

So this is why we're here, and we can read how all these spiritual blessings are received through the Father, and His Son Jesus, and the Holy Spirit.

Then, in the passage above, Paul prays for believers to receive 'the Spirit of wisdom and revelation', so that once received, we will be able to know God better, and with the eyes of our heart, we will be able to recognise what comes with God's plan – that is to say, the hope we are called to – which is the eternal life we are promised; the riches of our inheritance – which are all the blessings of the new creation we will share as adopted children of God; and His 'great power', which is given to every believer. This is the very same power that God used to raise Jesus from the dead and enthrone Him in heaven.

Paul refers to the eyes of our heart to mean our minds and inner understanding. To see things clearly, we need our hearts to be totally aligned with God's, so the Holy

---

[184] See Ephesians 1:3-6.

[185] See Ephesians 1:7-12.

[186] See Ephesians 1:13-14.

Spirit can reveal the truth and help us to understand. It is the Spirit who will explain everything to us, as we follow His lead and rely on His help.

Thoughts for reflection before we talk with God

God wants us to know about His purposes to have a family for Himself, and to have all creation united in Christ, and for us to be clear about what the Church is to do until that time comes, so God does want to talk with us.

Imagine being in a library with a good-sized world globe in it, with you sitting there, wondering why we're all here. You can turn the globe to see the countries of the world; perhaps you can see your favourite places, or some of the wonders of the world, or places you hope to visit. God's family will include people from all the nations of the earth, and you can see the countries spread across the continents, with different ethnicities, histories, languages, traditions, cultures and so much more. No nation is excluded from God's family, because the gospel 'will be preached in his name to all nations'[187] before the end of time.

Perhaps when you meet Jesus later, you can ask Him how His plan came to be, or when He knew He had to save the world from sin? Perhaps you may like to ask Him about the blessings promised to believers, and about the 'crown of righteousness'[188] which is in store for you. No question you can think of is unanswerable.

Christ is also appointed the head of the Church, and all believers in Jesus belong to the Church, so we all have a

[187] Luke 24:47.
[188] 2 Timothy 4:8.

part to play in the fulfilment of God's plan. The Church is built up when believers spend time with God in adoration, thanksgiving and praise and exhibit faith, love and service in the communities in which they live. Without the saving grace of Jesus, we would live our lives following our own agendas, habits and routines, but once we accept Jesus, we surrender our old lifestyle and take up a new life that honours God and our neighbours. Families will seek to live together in the way that Christ cares for the Church,[189] and believers will seek to live the Christian life by walking the way of love Jesus showed us.

What about our church life? Possibly Jesus might have something to say about this, perhaps asking us to take up a new role, or put down an existing one? Consider if there is something from our old lifestyle that needs His healing touch now. The Holy Spirit will help us to listen as God talks about our work in the church today, and in the world.

Paul prayed for the 'Spirit of wisdom and revelation' for the church in Ephesus, to be used for the common good, but there are other spiritual gifts and God equips us with those appropriate for our calling. Do you want to ask God which gift would be right for you? Have you asked for a gift and not received it? Perhaps God has given you a different gift instead?

The Bible tells us life on earth is a spiritual battle. Paul tells us, 'For our struggle is not against flesh and blood, but against the rulers, against the authorities, against the powers of this dark world and against the spiritual forces

---

[189] See Ephesians 5:29.

of evil in the heavenly realms.'[190] To protect ourselves, we can 'put on the full armour of God', which includes the 'helmet of salvation' to protect our head and our thinking, a 'breastplate of righteousness' to protect our hearts, a 'belt of truth' to help us discern truth from lie, our feet made ready by 'the gospel of peace', the 'shield of faith' to ward off the enemy's darts, and the 'sword of the Spirit, which is the word of God', for our reference and guidance.[191]

When you meet Jesus, why not talk about putting on the armour of God, about how to keep it in good repair, and what things might reduce its protective power? It is easy to be held captive by the world and lose sight of the eternal dimension. God does have a plan, and it will succeed in His timing, because the death and resurrection of Jesus made God's plan possible, and all of us who believe in Jesus have the power of God living in us to help us on our way.

The conversation

Imagine yourself now in the library with Jesus, standing together and looking at the world globe. When you first entered the room, He listened as you told Him about your hopes, or experiences, of visiting places in the world He made, and then He told you there is so much more He wants to say to you about our future with Him in eternity after the world ends. So as you settle down in easy chairs for your serious talk, why not let the Holy Spirit lead you

---

[190] Ephesians 6:12.
[191] See Ephesians 6:13-17.

into a conversation with Jesus about why we're here, and the future that God has in store for us.

A prayer to finish

Lord Jesus, thank You for explaining the plan for the world and my place in it. I have the promise of eternal life with You, and I am filled with the power of God that allows me to make a difference on earth. How amazing is that!

Thank You that I belong to the body of Christ. I pray that I will be useful and productive in the Church, and the world, every day. Amen.

28
There is No Condemnation

Therefore, there is now no condemnation for those who are in Christ Jesus, because through Christ Jesus the law of the Spirit who gives life has set you free from the law of sin and death. For what the law was powerless to do because it was weakened by the flesh, God did by sending his own Son in the likeness of sinful flesh to be a sin offering. And so he condemned sin in the flesh, in order that the righteous requirement of the law might be fully met in us, who do not live according to the flesh but according to the Spirit.[192]

The covenant law was introduced when Moses met God at Mount Sinai. God had said if Israel would obey Him and keep His covenant, 'then out of all nations', Israel would be God's special possession, 'a kingdom of priests and a holy nation'.[193]

Having shown His love for them when He had led them out of Egypt, the law would affirm them in their special relationship with God. The law was written down so they would know where the boundaries had been set, and when Moses told the people what God had said, and about the laws God was introducing to help them, the

---

[192] Romans 8:1-4.
[193] Exodus 19:5-6.

people had agreed. So sacrifices were made, the Book of the Covenant was read aloud, and the people confirmed they would be obedient to everything the Lord required.[194] By obeying God and the law and living a holy life, the people could become acceptable to God and He would live among them until the promise He gave to Abraham[195] was fulfilled through Jesus.

Sadly, the people could not meet the standards. It was not the law at fault – the law merely stated how to live a good, holy life – but the people were not capable of the obedience it required, and everyone sinned. The apostle Paul explains the problem in his letter to the Romans, in that he would not have known what sin was unless the law had told him, and once the law had identified what was sinful, human nature took over and made living in obedience to the law impossible.

Long ago in Eden, God said that disobedience led to death,[196] and so gave the law to help us, but Paul could see the paradox, that what was meant to bring life actually brought death.[197] Recognising his own weaknesses, he described himself a 'wretched man' and pondered how he could be rescued from certain death, or who would do the rescuing. Then Paul finds the answer to his own question. It is God who rescues him through Jesus Christ.[198]

By dying on the cross as the perfect, sinless human being, Jesus reconciled all humanity to the holy, righteous God. Through Jesus, 'the law of the Spirit' has replaced

---

[194] See Exodus 24:7.

[195] See Genesis 12:2-3.

[196] See Genesis 2:17.

[197] See Romans 7:7-10.

[198] See Romans 7:24-25.

'the law of sin and death',[199] and all who call on His name in faith will be saved. Condemnation has no hold any more, because Jesus has set us free. Salvation through grace means we share eternal life with God.

Condemnation from the devil is very powerful. Condemnation arises when we are told we are guilty, because once judgement is given, then we dread punishment. It is like carrying a great weight on our back which is too difficult to shrug off. In a world where judgements are handed out so quickly, frequently by people who don't know all the circumstances or facts, or who have their own agenda to meet, or are careless about the hurt or damage their judgements may cause, condemnation is a feeling known to almost everyone, and we need God to help us deal with it.

There's not much said about the devil these days, and many people deny his existence, but the Bible is clear about who he is and what he does. Denial doesn't change anything; instead, it allows him free rein in our lives. Yet the amazing reality is that we can escape from his power to condemn, because 'there is now no condemnation for those who are in Christ Jesus'.[200] Because Jesus took our faults, errors and sins to the cross, His followers do not have to bear hurtful accusations from the devil; we have been forgiven, and we have the power and authority to take action to escape condemnation when we get attacked.

If the voice of the devil tries to load us with condemnation, we can call on the name of Jesus and command the devil to be silent and to leave us, inviting

---

[199] Romans 8:2.
[200] Romans 8:1.

the Holy Spirit to fill us afresh as our words take effect. While our natural inclination may be to tell ourselves we deserve to be condemned, the Christian response can be different: we can escape what we deserve because of what Jesus has done – it's called grace.

Thoughts for reflection before we talk with God

Have you been made to feel guilty over a word spoken carelessly, by mistake or in haste, or for an action taken that you later regret? Does that carping voice in your head keep on repeating how awful you are, what a poor Christian you are, that you have let Jesus down, that you are a worthless friend and/or a bad Christian, and other such claims? It is easy to reach the bottom of a deep pit very quickly, and then it is difficult to escape. Sometimes it's too shaming or embarrassing to share it with a friend who could help. Sometimes we condemn ourselves the most.

Imagine Jesus joining you in the pit. He knows how you got there, and what you need to do to escape. The Spirit can explain the ways the devil uses condemnation to try to put distance between Jesus and His followers. We receive the Holy Spirit when we believe, and He explains how by grace we are forgiven our sin; He can teach us how to pray when condemnation strikes, and to recognise it when it creeps up on us.

Jesus gave His disciples 'power and authority to drive out all demons and to cure diseases'.[201] By the Spirit, we have the same power and authority. Sometimes we can be reluctant or hesitant to call on such power, but the Spirit

---

[201] Luke 9:1.

will encourage us and teach us, and the more we defend ourselves, the more effective we will become.

Resting in the power of the Spirit, let Him lead you in saying the words that rebuke the devil and all his works, and cancel out all condemnation. Jesus alone has authority to be our judge.

The conversation

Imagine meeting Jesus in a courtroom as you stand in the dock. You are found guilty by the judgemental voices in the world, but Jesus is telling you a different verdict, that He has taken the punishment, so you're free to go. As He opens the door to freedom, you step out, with your good name unsullied. Why not talk to Him while you are standing there together? The Holy Spirit has been beside you during the time of condemnation, so, resting in His strength, why not talk to Jesus about the lie that underpins condemnation, and about the power and authority God has given to His people to bring about their release and freedom?

A prayer to finish

Lord Jesus, by Your victory on the cross, my sins are forgiven and I am released from the weight of condemnation. Thank You for grace and life in the Spirit. Sometimes I still hear the voices of condemnation – but I trust Your promise to rescue me. You alone are my judge and I choose to live in the freedom You have won for me.

Lord, will You help me to live free from condemnation, and to tell of Your redeeming love to the people I share my journey with? Thank You. Amen.

29
Chariots and Horses

May the LORD answer you when you are in distress;
may the name of the God of Jacob protect you.
May he send you help from the sanctuary
and grant you support from Zion.
May he remember all your sacrifices
and accept your burnt offerings.
May he give you the desire of your heart
and make all your plans succeed.
May we shout for joy over your victory
and lift up our banners in the name of our God.
May the LORD grant all your requests.
Now this I know:
The LORD gives victory to his anointed.
He answers him from his heavenly sanctuary
with the victorious power of his right hand.
Some trust in chariots and some in horses,
but we trust in the name of the LORD our God.
They are brought to their knees and fall,
but we rise up and stand firm.
LORD, give victory to the king!
Answer us when we call![202]

---

[202] Psalm 20.

This psalm of David is a prayer for victory before battle is engaged. It begins with the people praying for the king as he gets ready to fight against a powerful enemy, that the Lord will protect him and make him victorious. David then joins the prayer and expresses his own belief that God will make him successful in battle. The people echo David's confidence and say that while 'Some trust in chariots and some in horses', God's people trust in the name of their Lord and therefore the enemy will be defeated, while God's people will take the victory. The psalm ends with the people repeating their prayer for the king's victory – trusting that God is faithful and that He will hear their prayer and act on it.

David is one of the memorable characters in the Old Testament. His life was packed with events that ranged from terrific success to total disaster. He was the youngest in a large family and was shepherding sheep in fields when he was chosen by God to be king of Israel in place of King Saul. God had sent the prophet Samuel to the house of Jesse to anoint one of his sons to be the next king, and David was identified as the one.[203] God explained the reason for His choice by saying He had found a man after His own heart.[204]

David came into service with King Saul because he played the harp well, and his reputation grew after he fought a Philistine warrior called Goliath and defeated him in battle, using his sling and a smooth stone.[205] He became friends with Jonathan, the king's son, lived at

---

[203] See 1 Samuel 16:1-13.

[204] See 1 Samuel 13:14 .

[205] See 1 Samuel 17.

court, married one of the king's daughters, and then had to defend himself against Saul's jealousy and many attempts to kill him. He lived on the run for a while, spared Saul's life more than once, and then composed a lament for Saul and Jonathan after hearing of their deaths on the battlefield.

As king, David won the civil war with the House of Saul, and thus all the tribes of Israel accepted David as their king. Thereafter he conquered Jerusalem, defeated the Philistines and other local tribes, disgraced himself with Bathsheba, and nearly lost his kingdom to his rebellious son Absalom, whom he mourned deeply when he was killed. He counted his fighting men against God's will and caused the plague that ravaged the people as a consequence, and he purchased the land on which the temple would be built in the future. After his death, his son Solomon became king and ruled over a golden age for Israel.

What a story – yet there was a thread that ran through David's life that was never broken: an indestructible faith in God as his strength, refuge, stronghold, leading light and redeemer.

David had status, power and immense wealth, including thousands of chariots and horses, but their existence did not prevent him knowing that God was more important than these. His times of hardships did not prevent his understanding that God was always with him, even when he couldn't feel His presence.

David made some very bad mistakes in his life that caused much suffering, but the pain did not drive him to abandon God; David always seemed to have the strength to dig deep in desperate days and say things like, 'But I trust in you, LORD',[206] or, 'But I will sing of your strength',[207] and to know God's love was constant. Despite his earthly riches, he had the wisdom to know that the chariots and horses under his control didn't compare with the power of God. When the outcome really matters, trusting in the Lord is the only sure way to proceed.

This prayer is relevant to us today. Do we have chariots and horses that we rely on – people or things we take for granted, which we do not recognise as representing the certainties we rely on in our lives? Perhaps we don't mention them to the Lord because they are so familiar to us? Individuals might rely on a big bank balance, or friends in high places, or politicians, or bolts on the doors and windows. Families sometimes rely on old traditions, or well-off relatives, family retainers, or professional advisers. Nations rely on armies, or a nuclear deterrent, or on treaties, sometimes with allies who are unreliable. Sometimes we can become our own chariots, relying on our own strength, wisdom and resources, not trusting God with the opportunity to help us. Of course, individuals need money, friends, protection and good advisers, and nations need Armed Forces and treaties, but where is our trust when the battle is fiercest?

Thoughts for reflection before we talk with God

Imagine hearing Jesus telling the parable about the rich fool with an abundant harvest, who built bigger barns to store his surplus,[208] or overhearing the conversation when

---

[206] Psalm 31:14.

[207] Psalm 59:16.

[208] See Luke 12:16-21.

a man asked Jesus what he should do to obtain eternal life and Jesus told him to sell everything and 'give to the poor'.[209]

Chariots and horses can come in all shapes and sizes. Do we have certainties in our life? They might be our wealth or possessions, or possibly the status from an appointment or a title we hold, or a job we do, or connections with particular people. When we meet Jesus, perhaps we could ask Him how they became more central to our security than we thought, even without really noticing. Sometimes they just grow up over time.

Or we could ask Him if we have become our own chariot, relying on our own wisdom. Sometimes we do this when we are afraid God will stop us from doing, having or getting something we really want. Yet the truth is that God's gifts are so much better than anything we could choose for ourselves. It is much better for us to trust Him, but if we find we have excluded Him, we can admit this and seek His forgiveness; He is full of grace, ready to forgive and forget.

The conversation

Imagine you're still in the crowd following Jesus and listening as He talks to the people. Now He has seen you in the crowd and makes a beeline to meet you. You find a quiet spot and you sit together. With the Spirit leading, perhaps ask Jesus if He sees you leaning on a chariot you did not know about, or if you are holding something very close to your heart which would be better shared with

---

[209] Mark 10:17-31.

Him, and then wait for His words of wisdom to make all things clear.

A prayer to finish

Dear God, I am sorry there are times when I choose to rely on worldly substitutes instead of trusting You. Thank You for showing me what they are, and encouraging me to turn my gaze back to You.

Help me, I pray, to trust You with all that I am, and with all that I have, that I may stand firm in my faith and not be tricked into leaning on false securities. I know Your promises are so much better than anything I can choose myself – grant me the courage, please, to be steadfast when I face the choices between what You offer me and what the world offers me. Thank You. Amen.

30
The Word

There remains, then, a Sabbath-rest for the people of God;
for anyone who enters God's rest also rests from their
works, just as God did from his. Let us, therefore, make
every effort to enter that rest, so that no one will perish by
following their example of disobedience.
For the word of God is alive and active. Sharper than any
double-edged sword, it penetrates even to dividing soul and
spirit, joints and marrow; it judges the thoughts and
attitudes of the heart. Nothing in all creation is hidden
from God's sight. Everything is uncovered and laid bare
before the eyes of him to whom we must give account.[210]

In the book of Hebrews, the author is encouraging
believers to do all they possibly can to obtain eternal life,
which he calls God's 'Sabbath-rest', and not to lose hope.

Life on earth can be very intense, sometimes causing
our perspective to become too small, so the Bible reminds
us that our existence here on earth is only part of the story
for God's people, and that there is life after death for those
who believe in Jesus. To ensure we obtain this, we are
urged to 'make every effort' to avoid the fate of the people
of Israel, who failed to enter into their Sabbath-rest (in this

---

[210] Hebrews 4:9-13.

context meaning the promised land) after their deliverance from slavery in Egypt. Owing to their disobedience and lack of faith, the people spent forty years in the desert, and during that time, all of those who had rebelled against God died.

To make every effort is not a call to earn our salvation, but a call to enter our Sabbath-rest by faith. To help us do this, we are directed to the written Word of God, the Bible; this is described as being 'alive and active', and sharp enough to divide our invisible innermost self – it can even divide our 'soul and spirit, joints and marrow' – while judging 'the thoughts and attitudes of the heart'. As we read the Bible, it convicts us of everything that is wrong in us, including our sins (where we break God's law to any degree, even if unintentionally), our transgressions (when we cross a boundary, intentional or not) and our iniquities (our intentional wickedness).

If we wonder how the Bible can judge our thoughts and attitudes and convict us of sin, we can reflect on a verse from John's Gospel which declares 'the Word was with God, and the Word was God'.[211] Jesus is both the Living Word and the Written Word.

Nothing can be hidden from God, because God is all-seeing, all-knowing, all the time, everywhere. The activity of the Word is Jesus Himself at work, by His Spirit, and the judging of what we think, and our attitudes, points ahead to the judgement that will occur at the end of the world.

The day of judgement is not referred to much these days, but it is a future reality. The book of Revelation

---

[211] John 1:1.

mentions the dead being present before God and each person being judged for what they have done in their lives; no one will be able to escape scrutiny, or deny what they have been seen to have done.[212]

The followers of Jesus, by faith and grace, will be named in the book of life and will enter God's rest. Conversely, the people who don't follow Jesus presumably risk suffering the same fate as the people of Israel. So our eternal future is inextricably linked to our attitude to the Bible, and we need to be mindful of this.

Thoughts for reflection before we talk with God

It is good for us to talk to Jesus about our relationship with the Bible. It is the indispensable guide to living the Christian life, a written reference, in many languages, that is visible, tangible and audible.

It is the surest way to check if we hear correctly from the Holy Spirit – there will never be a contradiction between what the Word says and what the Spirit says. If they don't seem to agree with each other, we must tread with much caution; either we may not have heard from the Holy Spirit after all; or if we are certain it is the Holy Spirit who has spoken, we may not have interpreted correctly what we have learned from the Spirit, or from the written text. Much wisdom and discernment is needed if Word and Spirit do not appear to agree.

It can be helpful if we consider what the Bible means to us. Is it an essential guide to our daily living, or is it more a reference work for a study paper we are writing? Do we limit our reading to the New Testament, or do we follow

---

[212] See Revelation 20:12-13.

how the prophecies in the Old Testament are fulfilled in the New Testament? Do we follow a designated reading pattern, so that we have the opportunity to read the whole Bible over a set period, or do we read a devotional that prints small extracts? Whatever we do, it's pleasing to God, but it's worth asking Him if we might use the Bible in other ways too.

We could ask God why we find some parts so difficult to understand, or even read sometimes. Or we could share some of the verses that mean so much to us. We could ask Jesus what to read. A benefit of reading or listening to all the books in the Bible is that we can meet the books that we don't know very well; then we can avoid choosing too often (perhaps unknowingly) the books or verses that we like, and missing out the parts that make us feel awkward, or challenge us. We could ask if it helps to read more than one version of the Bible and if so, why?

Jesus knows each of us so well; if we let Him direct our reading, He will help us grow in wisdom and understanding. Are we willing to let the Holy Spirit lead us on a new journey of discovery?

The conversation

Imagine Jesus sitting beside you in a comfy chair at home, a Bible in hand. Although He is the Living Word, He loves to use a written version of the Bible too, so it's like two friends sitting and discussing any good book. With the Spirit guiding your thoughts and words, you could ask Him about something that has arisen in your daily reading recently, or perhaps some other point about the written Word that the Holy Spirit is prompting you to ask, knowing it will bring you a deeper understanding, and a blessing too.

A prayer to finish

Dear God, You have given us Your Word so that we might know about You, Your majesty and Your character, and learn of Your compassion, love, mercy and grace throughout the pages of history. The Word reveals all Your promises for this life and the next. 'Your word is a lamp for my feet, a light on my path.'[213]

I pray, Lord, will You refresh my relationship with the Bible, that I might become familiar with its contents, and open to the Spirit as He seeks to make known all the good things You have prepared for the people who love You? Thank You. Amen.

---

[213] Psalm 119:105

Appendix
Crowhurst Christian Healing Centre

For more than ninety years the Lord Jesus Christ has used Crowhurst Christian Healing Centre (CCHC) to meet people at their point of need, with His peace, presence and power. Countless people tell stories of being rested, refreshed and renewed, inspired and guided, healed and transformed. This is the work of Jesus.

CCHC is situated in an Area of Outstanding Natural Beauty, providing a beautiful, comfortable and spacious place readily accessible by road and the close proximity of Crowhurst railway station. It is an ideal setting in which to draw closer to God and experience His love.

Residential and drop-in facilities are available for visitors to the centre who can choose from a variety of Retreats, Quiet and Teaching Days or just enjoy personal space. A rhythm of Christ-centred, Spirit-filled worship is available, alongside opportunities for creativity and prayer from the experienced team of compassionate ministers. The comfortable hospitality, pristine conditions and delicious meals all contribute to a truly healing experience.

The ministry of CCHC is available as a resource beyond the centre, having worked in a variety of Church and

Christian ministries around England and further afield, Israel (Nazareth) and Bulgaria. There is also provision to access CCHC resources on the internet through our website, YouTube and Facebook.

With a vision for the kingdom of God 'on earth as it is in heaven',[214] CCHC is daily saturated in and with prayer by passionate followers of Jesus, resulting in what some call 'a thin place'. It is truly unique.

Jesus says the kingdom of God is within us and 'has come near'.[215] The kingdom of God is very evident at CCHC where Jesus is King, the Holy Spirit is invited to have free rein and the Father's love is poured out day by day.

If you would like to know more about CCHC, please see our website: www.crowhursthealing.org.uk

If you are hungry and thirsty for a touch from the Lord, His invitation to you is 'Come and see'.[216]

---

[214] Matthew 6:10
[215] See Luke 17:21; Mark 1:15.
[216] John 1:46.